Global Democracy

The Struggle for Political and Civil Rights
in the 21st Century

I hope this inspires you !

Global Democracy

The Struggle for
Political and Civil Rights
in the 21st Century

Didier Jacobs

Vanderbilt University Press • NASHVILLE

© 2007 Vanderbilt University Press
All rights reserved
First Edition 2007

11 10 09 08 07   1 2 3 4 5

This book is printed on acid-free paper made
from 50% postconsumer recycled paper.
Manufactured in the United States of America
Designed by Dariel Mayer

Jacobs, Didier.
Global democracy : the struggle for political and civil rights
in the 21st century / Didier Jacobs.—1st ed.
p. cm.
Includes bibliographical references and index.
ISBN 978-0-8265-1572-8 (cloth : alk. paper)
ISBN 978-0-8265-1573-5 (pbk. : alk. paper)
1. Democracy. 2. Democratization. I. Title.
JC423.J24 2007
321.8—dc22
2007001301

For my mother Thérèse, who devoted her life to me and my family
For my father Luc, who helped me understand human nature
For Professor Ronald Heifetz, who helped me understand social change
For my teacher Jean-Pierre Boutez, who let me discover the world
For my wife Jae-Eun, who believes in me
And for my son Jérôme, may he live in a peaceful world

*There is no greater power than an idea
whose time has come.*
> Victor Hugo (1802–1885),
> French novelist and humanist

*Do unto others what you would have them
do unto you.*
> "The Golden Rule,"
> Matthew 7:12 and Luke 6:31

Institutions alone fix the destinies of nations.
> Napoleon Bonaparte (1769–1821),
> Emperor of France

Contents

Part III Applying Global Democracy

Global Democracy

The Struggle for Political and Civil Rights
in the 21st Century

Introduction

AT HIS 2004 STATE of the Union address, President George W. Bush said that there was no way the United States would accept that its foreign policy be dictated by foreigners, including the United Nations.[1] This statement was well attuned to American public opinion, and in fact his challenger, Senator John Kerry, had said much the same thing a month earlier, albeit more diplomatically.[2]

The reverse is true, too. There is no way the rest of the world will continue to let Washington make decisions that have vital consequences for the whole world, such as whether or not to denuclearize Iran by force. The pressure for Western countries to share power with the rest of the world will also continue to grow for more mundane global public policy decisions, such as regulating trade-distorting agricultural subsidies or defining international intellectual property rights.

The simple idea of global democracy—that all human beings should have equal say in decisions affecting the whole humankind—has already gained significant momentum. The charge against "democratic deficits" is at the heart of the global movement for social justice (sometimes called the "antiglobalization" movement), which has mobilized hundreds of thousands of demonstrators throughout the world. "This is what democracy looks like!" could be read on billboards in the streets of Seattle in 1999, where that movement crystallized in protest against closed-door negotiations among trade ministers of the wealthiest countries who meant to set trade rules for the whole world. Resistance against American unilateralism is also an important bond of the peace movement that reemerged to protest the war against Iraq. Even some people who are not activists are already familiar with the idea: I have heard some Europeans joking at cocktail parties that they ought to have the right to vote in American presidential elections because they are also affected by the result.

The incompatibility between President Bush's statement and the aspiration of many people for global political rights points to a major confrontation that is going to play itself out in the coming decades. To set the tone for this book, it is worth drawing an analogy with a similar confrontation that developed over a whole century in Britain. In the second half of the nineteenth century, Britain was a liberal democracy of sorts. Freedoms of expression and association were fairly extensive and protected by a robust legal system with independent judiciary. Parliament controlled government and was elected through competitive elections. But only wealthy men, a tiny proportion of the population, were eligible to vote. Britain was a highly stratified society. Rules were made by the wealthy to benefit the wealthy, making social mobility difficult. Not surprisingly, the disenfranchised did not like the situation. Workers went on strike and protested in the streets about their unfair living conditions. The middle class, which grew despite rigged rules, increasingly fretted about suffrage. Upper-class males, however, were convinced that universal suffrage would be folly, as "illiterate workers" and "irrational women" were not to be trusted in government. Yet after several decades of incremental reforms that made the franchise more inclusive,[3] they eventually had to capitulate in front of the masses' yearning for political equality. All males and some women gained the right to vote in 1918, all women in 1928, and equal universal suffrage (one person, one vote) was finally achieved when upper-class people lost their privilege of multiple votes in 1949. The Labor Party duly took over government for the first time in 1923 and ushered in the era of the welfare state. Eighty years later, social classes have not disappeared, but no one denies that British society is significantly more equal. The adoption of equal universal suffrage was not a revolution—political parties continued to alternate healthily in government—but probably was the single most important decision of Parliament to empower the working class and women.

We are in 2006 and world politics looks strikingly similar to nineteenth-century British politics. Despite remnants of despotism in parts of the world and arguments about civil liberties in the context of the so-called war on terror, freedoms of expression and association have never before been more extensive than they are today. The rule of law prevails, albeit not as strongly as it did in Britain: While transnational economic activities are regulated by a tight web of enforceable global rules, political leaders can still get away with crimes against humanity—although the web of international law is tightening in the former Yugoslavia, Rwanda, Iraq, Darfur, and Uganda. Global public policies are debated and decided by officials, not in a single parliament, but in a multiplicity of assemblies called intergovernmental organizations. As in nineteenth-century Britain, however, there is no political equality. Representatives of the United States and the European Union or its member-states invariably wield more power than representatives of other states. Unsurprisingly, they use that power to their interests: Trade rules are rigged against poor nations; Africans will be the last to be effectively protected from crimes against humanity.

WILL WORLD POLITICS FOLLOW the path of nineteenth-century British politics? This book argues that it should, and that it could. I will develop two reasons to advocate for global democracy. First, I will claim that political equality at the global level of government is a human right. "Do unto others what you would have them do unto you" is a universal moral norm, one that is part of many religious and cultural traditions.[4] Applied to world politics, it implies sharing power. I will explore what political equality can mean at the global level, and how it can practically be put in place.

The second reason to advocate for global democracy is that democracy has proved to the least bad way to govern for the common good. I will discuss how global democracy would be likely to alter global public policies given the current and foreseeable interests and preferences of major nations and transnational groups, and I will argue that such changes will be mostly for the better for humankind as a whole.

Likewise, I will develop three reasons to believe that global democracy is "an idea whose time has come," that it is a realistic (though by no means certain) outcome to expect in the coming decades. There are indeed three political forces that are developing under our eyes, the combination of which has already put in motion incremental change toward global democracy.

The first of these forces is the global movement for social justice: a grassroots movement of people who feel disenfranchised in world politics, are determined to have their voices heard, and are increasingly organized through a transnational network of civil society organizations. Many fine books have already been written on the development of global civil society, on the real power that it wields, and on how it could further develop.[5] Unlike most other books on global governance and global democracy, I am not going to dwell on the growth of global civil society but rather take it as a given. I will assume that Ann Florini's conclusion is right: Global civil society is here to stay.[6]

The second force is the rise of what one could call the "global middle class." I have particularly in mind the rising assertiveness of populous poor and middle-income nations in world politics, like Brazil, China, India, and Russia. Again, while one can speculate on the sustainability of this trend, it is reasonable to expect continued economic growth in Asia and other parts of the world over the coming decades, which would yield growth in political clout as well.

The third force is an enlightened faction of the "global upper class," which sees globalization as a process that is imperative to pursue not only to meet tomorrow's global challenges, such as feeding billions more people while preserving the earth's ecologic balance, but also simply to avoid reverting to a perverse cycle of nationalism and wars. That faction of liberal internationalists, of economic globalization enthusiasts, is very much at odds with the global movement for social justice, many members of which see economic globalization as the problem rather than the solution. However, faced with the opposition of that movement plus the rise of the global middle class, liberal internationalists are likely to accept compromise, to accept reform of globalization in order to save it, and, relating that to this book's topic, to accept the democratization of world politics in order to facilitate the negotiation of such compromises. This is all the more likely because liberal internationalists tend to be strong supporters of civil and political rights, and so should be natural supporters of global democracy.

The advent of equal universal suffrage in Britain rested on the same combination of political forces: angry labor activists in the streets, a rising middle class, and part of the elite, which, at the eleventh hour, preferred to share power and allow the emergence of reformed capitalism in order to avert socialist revolution. These three political forces are clearly discernible in world politics and are much better established today than they were only ten years ago. Their development over the decades to come makes global democracy an idea that can no longer be dismissed.

The ultimate purpose of this book is thus to set out a particular vision of global democracy around which disparate and even opposed political forces might eventually coalesce. That vision is anchored on one very familiar form of democracy: liberal representative democracy. My focus throughout this book is on political rights, particularly equal universal suffrage, and institutional reforms of intergovernmental organizations that are necessary to uphold these rights.

"Institutions alone fix the destinies of nations," Napoleon purportedly said. This statement applies to the destiny of the world as well. I am an economist, and as such I believe that individuals respond to incentives, and institutions are sets of incentives. Institutions hard-wire behaviors. By and large, we have the world we deserve—for better and for worse—based on the international institutions we have. Given human nature, I cannot imagine the world becoming a significantly better place without radically changing international institutions. Institutions are hard to change, but they do change. Throughout this book I will show how global democracy could develop based on institutional change that is already happening. The European Union will of course be exhibit number 1 to illustrate that change, but there are also institutional innovations happening at the global level of government.

Liberal representative democracy is often taken for granted these days, and most of the literature on democracy focuses on new ways in which citizens can participate in the political process above and beyond the voting booth. The same is true for the nascent literature on global democracy. While I commend efforts to enhance liberal representative democracy and encourage citizens' direct participation in shaping global public policies, I do believe that representative democracy with equal universal suffrage remains absolutely critical to democracy. Direct participation is a complement to, not a substitute for, representation. Hence my focus is on political rights and institutions.

However, I am not naive about institutions. They should not be conceived in abstraction from the underlying diversity of interests and power relations in society. I am very aware that legal rights for disadvantaged people require social struggles not only to be obtained, but also to be enforced. Civil society has an important role to play in empowering marginalized people to exercise their rights. This book should therefore be read in parallel with the literature on global civil society.

THIS BOOK IS ORGANIZED in three parts. I begin by discussing, in Part I, what democracy can actually mean at the global level of government. I reexamine the meaning of a series of terms that are critical to understanding global democracy, including the notions of "global village" and "global community," government and governance, federalism and confederalism, sovereignty, competences and subsidiarity, functionalism and regionalism, and, of course, democracy. The definition of global democracy that emerges from Part I is the application of key concepts of democracy as we know it at the national level to world politics, which would happen incrementally over several decades by developing institutional innovations already adopted by some international institutions.

To clearly position global democracy, I contrast it, in Part II, with the four other choices of world politics that are routinely distinguished by political analysts:

- Benevolent imperialism (the neoconservatives' agenda)
- Nationalism (the realists' agenda or "balance-of-power politics")
- Multilateralism (support for the current United Nations system)
- Localism (an agenda advanced by some members of the global movement for social justice)

I then present, in Chapter 12, the features of global democracy based on the analysis from Part I. My goal for Part II is not to make a comprehensive set of specific institutional reform proposals.[7] Rather, I mean to position global democracy as a general attitude toward foreign policy making, just as the four other choices identified above are generally recognized as coherent foreign policy approaches even though they are caricatures and people who are associated to any one of them do not necessarily agree on every policy question—nobody fits a box.

Finally, in Part III, I advocate for global democracy by arguing that it would help deal with the challenges of today's world, which I break down in four global public policy areas:

- Promotion of peace and security
- Promotion of civil and political rights
- Promotion of economic and social rights
- Protection of the global environment

Again, my goal is not to make a comprehensive set of specific policy recommendations. Rather, I explore how some major global public policies are likely to be altered under the global democratic approach, generally for the better but, for some people, sometimes for the worse, considering the existing interests and preferences of major nations and transnational groups. In reviewing each of these policy areas, I also sketch how global democracy could take shape in the coming decades based on the interaction of the three political forces I mentioned earlier: global civil society, governments of populous poor and middle-income countries, and the liberal internationalist elite.

I conclude by drawing take-away lessons for five different audiences: activists of the global movement for social justice, government officials of poor and middle-income countries, European federalists, American neoconservatives, and American Democrats.

Part I

Understanding
Global Democracy

1

Global Village
and Global Community

IT HAS BECOME A cliché that we live in a global village, that the world has shrunk, and that what is done in one country has repercussions on the other side of the planet. On the other hand, nationalism remains a very potent sentiment, few people regard themselves as global citizens, and many doubt that global citizenship could ever become a widely shared identity.

It is important to ascertain the existence of some sort of global political entity because any conversation on global democracy would be irrelevant if there were none. If we live in a global village but few of us feel part of a global community, is that a sufficiently strong foundation on which to build global democracy? I claim that it is enough. I am going to argue that there is a global political entity, which is characterized by apartheid. We all indeed live in a global village in which several communities are politically segregated according to the color of their passports (that is, their nationality) if not that of their skin. Since we cannot crisscross the village with Berlin walls, and since apartheid is unacceptable, I argue that we will just have to learn to become global citizens, and that that is possible.

The notion of "global village" is used in different contexts: social, economic, or cultural. In the political context of this book, I will use the phrase "global village" as a metaphor to describe the fact that human beings are subject to common, global laws. More precisely, I will call "global village" the set of public policies that affect most if not all people (or specific categories of people) throughout the world, whether those policies emanate from national or local governments, intergovernmental organizations, or even the private sector (such as industry codes of conduct or quasi-legal norms of the business or nonprofit sectors). The existence of such a global village has been extensively highlighted in the past fifteen years by the literature on globalization and particularly on global governance.[1] This literature asserts that nations are increasingly interdependent and that many public policy problems now transcend state boundaries. The key question of global governance is therefore who should set policy:

> What is the proper constituency, and proper realm of jurisdiction, for developing and implementing policy with respect to health issues such as AIDS or BSE (Bovine Spongiform Encephalopathy [or mad cow disease]), the use of nuclear energy, the harvesting of rain forests, the use of non-renewable resources, the instability of global financial markets, and the reduction of the risks of nuclear warfare? [. . .] At issue is the nature of constituency, the role of representation, and the proper form and scope of political participation.[2]

As defined, the global village has existed for centuries. It was already significant during the era of European colonialism, for instance, and acquired a new life with the creation of intergovernmental organizations in the early twentieth century. However, its density has definitely increased in the past fifteen years, thanks to both technological progress and the end of the Cold War, both of which have significantly increased international interdependence. International institutions (by which I mean institutions governing the relationships between sovereign states, such as intergovernmental organizations, treaties, and international customs) are more numerous and active than ever before. National public policies also increasingly affect people around the world, even when they are designed for the public of a single country.

For example, there is no global treaty on antitrust matters at this time, yet there is a de facto global competition policy, which the European Union and the United States set for the whole world. When two multinational companies want to merge, antitrust civil servants in Brussels and Washington assess whether the merger would, on balance, be beneficial to European and American consumers respectively (a larger, merged company may be beneficial because it could achieve economies of scale and some of the savings could be passed on to consumers, but it may also be harmful if the merged company is too big compared to its rivals and practices monopoly pricing). Multinational companies that ambition to have a truly global scale usually have a significant presence in the European or American markets because of their sizes and therefore need the blessing of the European or American authorities to merge. On some occasions, a proposed merger accepted in Washington was rejected in Brussels or vice versa, and it was in effect killed because the would-be merged company needed to be active in both markets. When a merger is accepted across the Atlantic, however, it becomes a fait accompli for the rest of the world. Other countries may be able to curtail the monopoly power of the merged company on their own markets, but their domestic companies would have to compete with a new behemoth on the global market, whether they like it or not.

The global village's density has also increased in that many public policies are now explicitly meant to apply uniformly across the world. In the past, although trade policy was decided in the framework of an inter-governmental organization, the General Agreement on Tariffs and Trade (precursor to the World Trade Organization), it was mainly meant to manage the interfaces between national economies. The main policy tool was import tariffs. One country's tariffs did impact on another country's companies. But tariffs served as valves allowing exchanges between national markets that were otherwise subject to different national economic policies. Each country could negotiate its own import tariffs à la carte to ensure consistency with national economic policy. While this remains the norm, the World Trade Organization now increasingly edicts rules, such as minimum intellectual property rights, that are meant to apply uniformly in all its member-states. They are meant to create a global market, not to manage the necessary minimum interfaces between national markets. Rules that apply uniformly across the globe are more readily perceived as global public policies.

What is remarkable about the last fifteen years is, more than the increased density of the global village itself, indeed the growing consciousness of its existence. The term "global governance" appeared only about twelve years ago, reflecting a new consciousness about living in a "global neighborhood" requiring global public policy.[3] That consciousness is not the privilege of political scientists, but is increasingly rooted in large segments of populations around the world. This is particularly true in the economic realm, as people are becoming conscious that their jobs are vulnerable to global public policy decisions.

Claiming new political rights flows from that consciousness. Very few people use the term "political rights" in the global context, yet the notion has already taken hold. People are conscious that they are affected by global public policies. They therefore feel stakeholders of these policies and want a voice in shaping them, whether or not they are citizens of the state—if it is a state—that introduced a given policy. For some, claiming global political rights is a natural corollary of the consciousness of being affected by global public policies. For others, especially for people who have not been accustomed to democracy at the national level, it is more of a leap. For most people, the consciousness is very vague as they cannot necessarily name either the global public policies of which they feel a stakeholder or the institutions that decided those policies. It is also very limited, as they are conscious of only a fraction of all the aspects of their lives that are affected by global public policies. But for a minority of active citizens around the world, that consciousness is both better informed and more encompassing. They can see global public policies as a system that affects not only themselves but everyone. They know intimately that they live in a global village.

People's consciousness about the global village is what drives the call for global democracy. The right to participate in global public policy decisions will become a human right when it is first claimed and then widely recognized as such. The claiming has started and the recognizing is likely to follow in due course. The human rights that are now enshrined in the Universal Declaration of Human Rights (which includes political rights at the national and lower levels of government only) emerged in the same way. In a sense, women and men, or blacks and whites, had a moral claim to civil and political equality ever since the dawn of humankind. But it was only in the Enlightenment era that some people became aware of that intrinsic equality, only in 1945 that human rights were enshrined in a universal declaration, and only recently that human rights brushed away other philosophical foundations to the margins of world politics. Likewise, nationals of poor and rich countries, of weak or mighty ones, have had a moral claim to political equality in shaping global public policies ever since the global village took shape, but it is only very recently that a critical mass of people have become conscious of that claim—and it would take another few decades before global democracy would be enshrined into most international institutions.

WHILE MOST AUTHORS OF the global governance literature would accept the existence of a global village, they would at the same time assert that there is currently no global community.[4] The notion of political community refers to a sense of togetherness and solidarity shared by all members of a given society, thanks to which they consent to observe their government's rules even when they do not agree with them, for the sake of the common good and in exchange for the guarantee that other members of society will do the same. The observance of laws is of course strengthened by sanctions against the deviants, but the idea is that government, and certainly democratic government, would not be possible without citizens accepting their roles and responsibilities as members of a given political community.

A political community is not absent at the global level. It is manifest in the proliferation of transnational networks of civil society organizations, and of the support that ordinary citizens lend to these organizations. It exists, it is growing, but its emergence does lag behind the rapid development of the global village and behind the growing consciousness of the global village's existence.

On paper, we already have a strong global community. The United Nations' Charter asserts that "we the peoples" will cooperate to solve all the world's problems. The Universal Declaration of Human Rights makes the bold assertion that every human being is equal. Most national politicians, particularly in the West, would not dare declaring publicly that the claim is not true, that some humans are worth more than others. Yet that is unfortunately what their decisions reveal. The international community has spent an estimated $2 to $6 per beneficiary on emergency assistance to save the lives of civilians affected by various conflicts or natural disasters in Africa in 2000 (against a peak of $19 for Rwanda in 1995).[5] This compares with about $47 for Kosovars the year before. White Europeans just seem to be worth more than black Africans. At the other extreme, Western governments will spend whatever it takes to rescue their own nationals in any emergency situation. Similarly, I recall that the American press paid about as much attention to the fate of three American soldiers captured by Serbian forces during a week of the Kosovo war of 1999 as it did to the three hundred thousand ethnic Kosovar refugees who were on the road that week. This reveals that, in the eyes of the American press and public, the life of one American was worth about the same as that of one hundred thousand ethnic Kosovars. And the life of one Rwandan was worth nothing at all in 1994. Considering such shallow and unequal solidarity among peoples across the world, it is hard to imagine the blossoming of a cohesive global community in the near future.

The philosopher Peter Singer has powerfully argued that we human beings really are one community.[6] Even if we do not always feel that way, we ought to feel that way. But the ethical case for nurturing a global community does not stop there. Acknowledging the existence of a global village without a global community is resigning oneself to accepting global apartheid: a village within which different communities are intertwined yet politically segregated (in this case, along nationality instead of racial lines) and where minority communities impose rules on the majority.[7] In the absence of a global village, the absence of a global political community would be less problematic. Singer's argument notwithstanding, each national community could go about its affairs without concern for others. But the fact that so many actions of one such community can purposefully or inadvertently harm others makes the situation more problematic. The problem is therefore not only that rich nations give relatively little assistance to save the lives of nationals of poor countries, however unethical that is. The problem is also that powerful nations, in order to cope with problems that concern all nations, set global public policies that fit their own interests but sometimes harm less powerful nations.

Since apartheid is plainly unacceptable, the emerging global community must be strengthened. People throughout the world must learn to become members of a new political community—while simultaneously remaining members of their local, national, and regional communities. Thousands of civil society organizations are already educating the public in that regard. And this book seeks to sharpen the understanding of what being a member of the global community entails.

However, again because apartheid is plainly unacceptable, measures to introduce global democracy should not be postponed until the global community becomes stronger. We need global democracy not just because people increasingly start feeling like members of a global community, but because they live together in the same global village and step on each other's toes. The driver of global democracy is the consciousness of the global village, not so much the existence of a vibrant global community.

It is possible to build global democracy on the basis of a weak global community, provided that it is done incrementally. I should probably reveal at this point some of my personal history that has shaped my thinking on global democracy. I was born with one nationality, Belgian. I have since acquired two additional national identities: European and Walloon (technically, only my Belgian and European nationalities appear on my passport). In the early 1990s, the Kingdom of Belgium went through a double devolution process. It amended its constitution to become a federal state with Wallonia as one of its federated entities, and acceded to a new European treaty that transformed the European Union into something quite similar to a federal state as well. It is well possible that I will lose my original nationality before the end of my life, as Belgium might split up in very much the same way as Czechoslovakia did. Like many Europeans, I feel comfortable with these multiple identities, even if I did not particularly feel Walloon prior to devolution. The point here is that institutions do influence identities and that identities can therefore change with institutions.

Of course, I realize that my case is exceptional. But in a historical perspective, it is the norm rather than the exception. Most existing nation-states were created artificially, through wars and marriages between aristocrats. In some cases, new states consisted of one big nation absorbing smaller ones. In other cases, especially in Africa, state boundaries were drawn by the colonial power without regard to the geographic distribution of national groups. One way or the other, citizens learned to belong to their new state and develop a new national identity, generally over long periods of time. (The United States is one of the exceptions in that regard, as a sense of American identity separate from British identity drove the 1776 revolution.) Substate national or local identities have often continued to thrive despite the strengthening of the nation-state, forcing some nation-states to devolve power back to subnational federated entities (e.g., Britain and Scotland, Spain and Catalonia). In a very few cases, subnational sentiments prevailed and nation-states dissolved peacefully (e.g., Czechoslovakia, Soviet Union) or through civil war (e.g., former Yugoslavia, Eritrea). The norm, though, is that artificially created states have managed to become nations while allowing existing subnational and local identities to thrive, producing multiple national identities and allegiances.

The big difference between this historical perspective and my own Belgian and European experience is the absence of violence in the latter. Global democracy, if it is to be true to its liberal roots, ought to be not only nonviolent, but completely voluntary. It should only add rights and identities for people, not subtract them. That is, people should gain new opportunities to make their voices heard, but their rights to speak their own language or observe their religion should not be impaired in any way, for instance.

Whether violent revolutions are ever justified is an ethical question that is beyond the scope of this book. Historical evidence shows that most democracies have developed incrementally and peacefully through long periods of time, although with occasional spurts of violence. The French Revolution was perhaps the most brutal attempt to impose democracy by force and quickly. But, precisely because of its brutality, it did not produce an immediately sustainable democratic outcome. The American Revolution, by contrast, was much more an independence war than a revolution, as American states and towns had already laid the building blocks of democracy. Its outcome therefore held ground. If the global apartheid were as oppressive and left as little room for peaceful dissent as the 1789 French monarchy did, revolution might be an avenue to explore. But the better analogy is late nineteenth-century Britain, as some elements of global democracy already exist and others are developing through slow, incremental change. The best strategy to achieve global democracy is therefore to continue that trend, peacefully.

The example of the European Union provides a good illustration of how a global community could develop. Its institutions were created by the political elites of its original member-states at a time when the feeling of Europeanhood was no deeper or more concrete than the feeling of global citizenship is today. Once in place, European bureaucrats worked for several decades to develop a sense of togetherness among Europeans, both objectively by establishing a common heritage of laws and symbolically through civic education—or some would say propaganda. The result is that most Europeans now do feel that Europeanhood is part of their identity, whether that is a small part next to their national identity or a bigger one.

On several measures (e.g., penetration of international media and uniformization of pop culture, English as lingua franca), one could argue that the world is actually more integrated today than Western Europe was when the European Economic Communities (precursor to the European Union) were created in 1957. Moreover, a worldwide poll shows that cosmopolitan identity is not more pervasive in Europe today than it is in the rest of the world.[8] Only 13 percent of Europeans say that they primarily belong to the world or to their continent, which is slightly below the world average. Cosmopolitanism is more prevalent in the Americas and less in Africa (although one could add that anticosmopolitanism is also more prevalent in the United States, where nationalism thrives[9]). More interestingly, cosmopolitanism is significantly more prevalent among the younger generations. If the twentieth century's trend continued into the twenty-first century, the primary allegiances of the world's people born in the 2040s would be equally divided: A third would feel primarily citizens of the world or of their continents, a third would feel primarily citizens of their nation-state, and the last third would identify themselves first of all with their locality or town. Current trends might not continue, but they may just as well accelerate: Globalization has only been gathering pace in the past fifteen years. At any rate, the European benchmark seems to indicate that there is enough cosmopolitanism in the world to start building global democracy today—and indeed, that is what is happening.

That said, the recent debacle of the European constitution has revealed that the European political debate actually remains largely a collection of national debates mediated by the political elites of each country.[10] Those national elites cannot drive institutional integration endlessly without the people sharing a strong common identity. The development of global democracy can precede and pull that of a global community, but only so much. They will progress hand in hand, through incremental change over several decades.

2

Government and Governance

ACCORDING TO MOST DICTIONARIES, "governance" is pretty much synonymous with "government." But in the fields of political science and international affairs, the phrase "global governance" has become a catchphrase that is insidiously ideologically loaded. I am going to show that this phrase arguably represents the most serious challenge to the idea of liberal representative democracy.

Having established that there is a global village, the issue now is to determine how it could be governed legitimately. The political science literature of the past fifteen years has offered at least three paradigms to answer that question.

The first paradigm is world federalism. This paradigm makes a clear distinction between intergovernmental organizations and world government, and advocates the latter. In his book *World Federation?*, for instance, Ronald Glossop associates world government with the concepts of federation, shared sovereignty between the world government and its member-states, lack of secession rights for member-states, ability to tax, and ability of citizens to sue the world government and be sued by it.[11] By contrast, he associates the United Nations and other intergovernmental organizations with the opposite concepts of confederation, lack of sovereignty, existence of secession rights for member-states, lack of taxation power, and lack of direct legal relationships with citizens (as only states are subjects of international law). He then argues that, due to these characteristics, a world government would be both more legitimate and effective at making global public policy than the United Nations is. World federalism is thus definitely a prescriptive paradigm, not a descriptive one.

World federalism has a long history and was particularly popular in the aftermath of the Second World War and early Cold War as a reaction to the horrors of war and fear of a nuclear holocaust.[12] At the end of the Cold War, when the geopolitical situation had become the least unfavorable ever for world federalism, this paradigm paradoxically lost whatever remained of its momentum. Today, world federalism remains synonymous with utopia, at a time when utopia has lost its romantic cachet. The basic problem with world federalists is that they have not been able to articulate intermediate steps between the world they live in and the world they dream of.

WORLD FEDERALISM WAS SUPPLANTED by the "governance without government" paradigm, which was articulated by political theorist James Rosenau just after the Cold War.[13] The "governance without government" paradigm can be summarized in four tenets.[14] First, governance in the global village is exercised through many global actors, and private actors can be as important as public authorities. Public authorities include local and national governments as well as intergovernmental organizations; private actors include businesses and civil society organizations broadly defined as nonprofit organizations, including the press, industry and professional associations, labor unions, religious organizations, academia, political parties, issue-based campaigning groups, and nonprofit social-services providers. Neither type of global actor must necessarily be based in multiple countries, although they are typically part of transnational networks, but they belong to the global village to the extent that some of their decisions have global repercussions.

Second, there is no central authority in the global village—no world government. This tenet is a direct rebuttal to world federalism.

Third, despite the lack of central authority, there are rules—there is governance. Global actors generate rules and apply pressure on each other in a variety of ways in order to have these rules respected. Compliance to rules is thus often voluntary (although states are global actors, too, and they do have coercive means to ensure compliance). While many global actors attempt to set rules in the global village, only some succeed, and Rosenau defines governance as the capacity to obtain compliance (or to govern) in the absence of legal authority.

Fourth, the atomization of power among a large number of actors is a new form of democracy, as any global actor acts as a check on the power of the others. Unlike the other three, this fourth tenet makes "governance without government" a prescriptive paradigm (because democracy is good), though it is not always articulated as such.

The "governance without government" paradigm gained popularity in the wake of the globalization phenomenon of the late 1990s, when everyone started to realize the burgeoning influence of transnational networks, fueled in part by technological progress and in part by liberal public policies loosening the grip of states on their economies. It has now acquired tremendous influence. Many leaders of civil society organizations, businesses, and intergovernmental organizations in particular do see the world in light of this paradigm, and so do many political scientists.

The best illustrations of the "governance without government" paradigm in action are the fashionable imperatives of "multistakeholder processes," "public-private partnerships," or "corporate social responsibility" to solve just about every global public policy problem. Multistakeholder processes are ad hoc and nimble institutions whose members emanate from the three big categories of global actors: governments (including intergovernmental organizations), businesses, and civil society (especially campaigning groups or service-delivery organizations). The processes are constituted to deal with narrow public policy problems and usually have a temporary lifespan. Their products are norms that are voluntarily adopted (or not) by relevant actors such as national governments or businesses. The idea is that the participatory decision-making process would give the norms some legitimacy—or expose those who ignore them to the wrath of campaigning groups. One of the first and best-known examples of multistakeholder process is the World Commission on Dams, which was meant to tackle the delicate problem of arbitrating the electricity needs of developing nations with the interests of the people displaced by large hydroelectric dams.[15] It was established when the World Bank could no longer deal with campaigning groups' opposition to the large dam projects that it was financing.

Public-private partnerships are institutional or informal collaborations between at least one governmental and one nongovernmental (business or civil society) actor. Like multistakeholder processes, they tend to focus narrowly on one public policy issue, but unlike them, their primary purpose is not to set norms but to deliver services, create new technologies, or build infrastructure. They are meant to combine assets of the public sector—authority and legitimacy—with those of the private sector—financial resources, expertise, and results-oriented attitude. A very high-profile example of a public-private partnership is the Global Fund to Fight HIV-AIDS, Malaria, and Tuberculosis, which is funded by the philanthropist Bill Gates, among others, and has become a substitute for the United Nations itself to fight the global scourges of HIV-AIDS, tuberculosis, and malaria. Both multistakeholder processes and public-private partnerships have proliferated in recent years.

The third fashion consistent with the "governance without government" paradigm is corporate social responsibility, which pits campaigning groups against businesses—two private actors—to shape industry codes of conducts regarding social and environmental issues.[16] Campaigning groups pressure businesses by tarnishing their brands. Their power is derived not from government authority but from the appeal of their ethical arguments and their effectiveness in public relations. Many campaigning groups have found it easier to serve their social or environmental missions by pressuring businesses than by relying on the old-fashioned strategy of influencing government policies.

For example, the pharmaceutical industry has been under heavy pressure to lower drug prices in poor and middle-income countries in order to increase poor people's access to lifesaving drugs. The alternative, state-centric way to achieve the same goal would have been to pressure governments of rich countries to dramatically increase their financial contributions to United Nations agencies, which could then have bought drugs at the full price and distributed them to poor countries at a fraction of the cost. Campaigning groups figured out that pressuring businesses was much easier. Pharmaceutical companies, which unlike tobacco or weapons manufacturers fulfill an essentially positive social purpose, quickly became villains and had no choice but to revisit their pricing policies.[17]

This example shows that there is enthusiasm and energy behind the "governance without government" paradigm even among the most progressive global actors. However, leaders of the global movement for social justice do not fully buy that paradigm. They use it for expediency's sake. They accept it as a descriptive paradigm, but not as a prescriptive one. When asked about the kind of world they yearn for, they insist on the importance of the state. They are aware of the danger that their own actions can undermine the state. And they see the need for a stronger and more legitimate global authority: A survey shows that two-thirds of nongovernmental organizations' leaders would favor an "evolving world government with global institutions accountable to citizens."[18]

EVEN FOR DESCRIPTIVE PURPOSES, the "governance without government" paradigm may not be as useful as it seems. Each of its tenets can be deconstructed, and in the end one may wonder whether there is any real difference between "government" and "governance." The first tenet—the multiplicity of actors and importance of the private sector—is neither new nor proper to the global level of government. Both businesses and civil society organizations have always influenced each other as well as the state. The state itself has never been monolithic at the national level either. It is a collection of bodies that share authority—and indeed are meant to compete with each other—including town, county, state, and federal governments; legislative, judicial, and executive branches; and executive branches' departments and autonomous, quasi-public agencies.

The third tenet—the importance of self-compliance—is not new either. Many essential national norms have either never been enshrined into laws or have been enforced by self-compliant citizens and companies with little or no necessity for police and courts. The International Chamber of Commerce, a business association, has been setting norms and standards and arbitrating disputes since 1919, and there were national and local chambers of commerce before that, for instance. While there is a clear trend toward self-regulation of the private sector (exemplified above with the corporate social responsibility vogue), it does not require changing the way we conceive of government. It is a trend that elected governments have allowed to develop and that they could take back—the notion that globalization has rendered national governments unable to regulate their national economies has been overplayed, at least for large countries.

The second tenet—the absence of a central authority at the global level—is misleading. The United Nations, including all its more-or-less autonomous agencies, can be described as a world government. The essential characteristic of government, according to political scientists, is the monopoly of violence. The United Nations has that characteristic: Despite the right of each member-state to maintain an army for self-defense, its Security Council is the only body entitled to authorize the use of force by states. The fact that it has used that authority only sparingly in the midst of uncontrolled violence emanating from states and nonstate actors suggests that it is an ineffective government but does not contradict that it is a government. Its lack of effectiveness, in turn, does not result from a lack of power. The five permanent members of the Security Council have a combined military force by and large sufficient to enforce world peace. The problem is that they are unable to resolve disagreements among themselves about the way to achieve world peace. Our world government is ineffective at maintaining world peace because of a very inflexible decision-making rule: the veto right. The current state of the world—mostly peace with some hot spots and arms races—could be described as what the Security Council's permanent members collectively want it to be—a little like a bad compromise struck by political parties that find themselves bound to govern together in dysfunctional parliamentarian democracies.

Moving from political science to plain common sense, the United Nations is a government in the sense that it is an organization that does public policy. It looks like a government, with its offices, civil servants, and bureaucratic structures. It behaves like a government, gathering information, analyzing public policy problems, drafting and negotiating regulations, controlling the implementation of those regulations, and spending tax money on numerous programs. It does have coercive means to ensure compliance, from withdrawing funds to, in effect, declaring war. And it influences all people's lives in many concrete ways like a government, from providing refugees with vital supplies to ensuring a safe trip to anyone who boards an international flight.

It is interesting that we do not call the United Nations "our world government." Common English usage includes the phrases "local governments," "state governments," and "federal governments," but refers to international public authorities as "intergovernmental organizations," "international institutions," or "international organizations." As these institutions' importance is gaining increased recognition, people are using more and more convoluted terms to refer to them, like "institutions of global governance" or "system of global governance." On the other hand, the simple phrase "world government" is reserved for world federalist utopias. One possible explanation of this usage may be that people associate the word "government" with the notion of sovereignty. But that does not make sense, because local governments are not sovereign either. They are as much creatures of states as intergovernmental organizations are, yet we do not call them "local institutions" or "intragovernmental organizations."

I suspect that the avoidance of the word "government" in the global context stems from the close association between the notions of government and democracy, at least in Western countries where all these terms have been shaped. Let us imagine for a moment that the United Nations General Assembly were composed of representatives directly elected by the people, and that it had some kind of real power—say, codecision on all matters currently dealt with by the Security Council, the International Monetary Fund, the World Bank, and the World Trade Organization. Then most people would probably agree that the United Nations is their world government. The United Nations could remain a patchy set of autonomous organizations; it would not need any additional transfer of competences from states; its authority could still be challenged by some governments and private actors; it could spend exactly the same budget and its regulatory powers might not be increased at all. If only there were high-stake elections, people would recognize it as their government—whether they liked it or not.

But elections are not a defining feature of government. Democracy is only a form of government. What we have at the global level is another form of government, characterized by apartheid. "Global governance" is a euphemism hiding the lack of democracy at the global level of government. Encouragingly, people are becoming increasingly aware of the power of their world government, and the phrase "global government" is now increasingly common—"world government" has kept the stigma of an overbearing superstate.

This leads us to the fourth tenet of the "governance without government" paradigm—the atomization of power as a new form of democracy. This tenet is also misleading. While it is true that a huge number of actors have a slice of power in the global village, at the end of the day power remains heavily concentrated in the U.S. government and its European allies. While the United Nations' agencies form the government apparatus that formally approves many if not all global public policies and implements them, power within that government is held by a small club of states centered on the North Atlantic axis.

Rosenau argues that the United States does not have a monopoly of power in the world.[19] That is correct. However, there is a continuum between atomization and monopolization of power. Within that continuum, it is fair to say that the United States and its European allies together wield hegemonic power (and it would not be far-fetched to use that term for the United States alone). I will argue that the West's power has started to decline relative to that of the rest of the world, and this decline is one of the forces on which global democracy could be built. Meanwhile, the U.S. government continues to wield tremendous influence on just about every global public policy issue. The terrorist attacks of September 11, 2001, have revealed that, when its vital interests are at stake, Washington can either act unilaterally or through "alliances of the willing" in defiance of international law, such as with the invasion of Iraq, or harness the support of the international community to push through far-reaching reforms, such as stricter controls on the movement of people and capital, to fight terrorism. In fact, the first administration of George W. Bush has belied the "governance without government" paradigm. President Bush has gone about pushing his foreign policy agenda through old-fashioned state-to-state diplomacy, and has not shied away from a command and control attitude. While it is true that he has reverted to a more multilateral approach in his second term, having realized that going it alone entails costs, the claim that power is atomized in the global village is almost ludicrous.

The "governance without government" paradigm is thus of limited use as a tool to understand world politics. It is not a good basis on which to build a project of global democracy. Before turning to the third paradigm that allows thinking about governing the global village, it is necessary to delve in more depth into the notion of democracy itself. If not atomization of power among a large number of actors, what is democracy?

3

Democracy

DEMOCRACY IS RULE BY the people. Everyone knows how it works, and that it does not work perfectly. Yet if we are to believe proponents of the "governance without government" paradigm, it is doomed. I believe that we are better off abandoning the seductive new political theory and continuing—indeed extending—our proven democratic practice.

Representative democracy, involving elections with equal universal suffrage, has proved a practical way of giving power to the people. And since "the people" is a diverse group, majority rule has historically emerged as the most legitimate and practical way to resolve political disagreements. Unanimity rule, or consensus-based decision making, may appear as more desirable because it ensures that nobody gets harmed by any decision. But it gives a veto right to the proponents of the status quo, allowing privileged people to preserve their privileges regardless of the common good. Majority rule levels the playing field, by making each vote count the same, while unanimity rule gives all the power to those— or the one person—who likes the status quo.

Majority rule and elections of representatives with universal equal suffrage are by no means all there is to democracy. Other crucial elements include freedom of expression and transparency of information by government agencies, freedom of association and an active civil society, quality civic education, an independent judiciary and the effective and impartial enforcement of laws, adequate codes of conduct in key professions such as law and journalism, and the endorsement by most members of society of the constitutional check-and-balance mechanisms limiting the scope of majority rule (e.g., fundamental freedoms, rights of ethnic minorities) and of the distribution of competences (or authority) among different levels of government, from towns to the federal level.[20]

However, proponents of the "governance without government" paradigm assail this received wisdom and tend to make a big leap from the correct premise that elections are not all there is to democracy, to the daring and logically flawed conclusion that global democracy can be obtained without elections at the global level of government. In an attempt to reconstruct the concept of democracy to fit at the global level, some political scientists are actually deconstructing it—and that has started to undermine democracy at the national level as well. This trend has been particularly powerful in recent years because it is relayed by both the center and the left of the political spectrum (the right being uninterested in the subject).

In the center, Rosenau and other authorities on global governance who are both academics and practitioners, like Joseph Nye of Harvard University, Anne-Marie Slaughter of Princeton University, or Ann Florini and Wolfgang Reinicke of the Brookings Institution, start by quickly dismissing representative democracy as impractical at the global level of government, emphasize that democracy is imperfect at the national level anyway, oversell what the "governance without government" paradigm has to offer in terms of democratic control, and conclude by acknowledging that what they propose may not be as democratic as what we are used to while inviting us to put up with the loss.

The book *Global Public Policy: Governing without Government?* by Reinicke illustrates this trend.[21] While calling for a reduction of the "democratic deficit," he invites us to "be careful not to reject all solutions that fall short of an ideal model of democracy, which does not exist and never has existed even at the domestic level." This statement belittles the tremendous progress toward "ideal" democracy that has been achieved over the past four centuries, from the civil rights movement in the United States to the end of apartheid in South Africa, from the working-class struggle to get the vote to the suffragette movement, from the collapse of communism in Eastern Europe to the end of military regimes in Latin America and elsewhere. More recently, the American presidential elections of 2000 and 2004 have indeed illustrated both the imperfection and the revered value of elections in democratic societies, and the profound attachment of the American people to the equal worth of each vote.

Having implicitly discarded elections as impractical at the global level, Reinicke seeks nonideal ways to tackle the democratic deficit. He suggests decomposing public policy into its three stages: agenda setting, decision, and implementation. National governments, which are democratic, could take care of the implementation of global public policies, and some degree of national idiosyncrasy should be allowed to subsist even at the cost of slight international frictions. Civil society organizations could play an important role at the agenda-setting stage, mitigating the democratic deficit through extensive consultation. But the decision stage would remain dominated by negotiations between states, that is, by balance-of-power politics. Yet the decision stage is of course crucial. As long as powerful states can block policy proposals, increasing participation at the agenda-setting stage is of limited use. Radical policy options, like the creation of global taxes to pay for global antipoverty programs, are regularly left out of the agenda because they are deemed unrealistic in the sense that they would be hard to sell to the American or European publics, not in the sense that they would be impossible to implement once adopted. Reinicke himself acknowledges the shortcomings of this arrangement in his conclusion:

> Global public policy will not necessarily erase the danger of a democratic deficit. On the contrary, [. . .] global public policy runs the risk of undermining popular sovereignty and thus the democratic character of policymaking even further. Thus it is of central importance to understand that globalization has led to a situation where democratic theory and the concept of pluralism can no longer be operationalized exclusively in the context of a territorially defined polity. Democratic governance must instead find new avenues, institutions, and instruments that reach beyond the current political geography of the nation state.[22]

This quote echoes a statement by Rosenau:

> How to subject decision-makers [in the global village] to a modicum
> of accountability and responsibility? How to ensure the liberties
> of individuals [. . .]? [. . .] Concepts of representation and
> accountability based on long-established territorial democracies
> in countries, provinces or cities ought not to serve as the basis for
> pondering the foregoing questions. [. . .] Rather, imagination and
> flexibility are needed if the dynamics that sustain the politics of this
> emergent domain are to be assessed in terms of their susceptibility to
> democratic control.[23]

Unfortunately, what he has to propose as substitute to elections and the
rule of law is pretty thin: competition among a large number of actors
who each have a slice of power, with a call for more active civil society
organizations and social movements; transnational networks of cities;
and the Internet as a tool to facilitate all of the above—all things we already have.

As the last two quotes suggest, the "governance without government"
paradigm unties the concepts of democracy and territoriality. According
to the conventional conception of democracy, public policies are made
by representatives of people living in particular territories and are enforced on those same territories. Proponents of the "governance without
government" paradigm claim that because decisions of global actors can
affect people living in distant corners of the earth—without necessarily
affecting their immediate neighbors—territories can no longer be used to
determine who should be involved in decision making.

However, this argument confuses the notion of public interest with
that of stakeholder participation. The public interest consists of all issues
that are legislated on in agreement with a country's (or territory's) constitution. It thus excludes issues that are left to the private domain, some
of which are protected by constitutional bills of rights (e.g., the right to
observe any religion). The public interest stems from the notion of stakeholder participation, as issues that are legislated on are generally those
that actually affect many people or potentially affect all people (e.g., the
prohibition against smoking in public). However, according to the con-

ventional conception of democracy, issues that are deemed of public interest by the people of a given territory do not necessarily affect all of them, and they certainly do not affect all of them to the same degree (e.g., regulations of recreational yachting). Nevertheless, people living on that territory all get one vote to legislate on them through their representatives, whether affected a lot, a little, or not at all.

While the notion of stakeholder participation makes sense in theory—those and only those who are affected by a decision should have a say in decision making—the notion of public interest is the only pragmatic way to apply it. The latter is well accepted at the local, state, and national levels of government. Contrary to what proponents of the "governance without government" paradigm claim, there is no reason why it could not be used at the global level as well, using the whole world or any subset of states as the territory of reference. So the proper constituency to regulate, say, the prevention of epidemic diseases like SARS could simply be the representatives of the states that choose to enter into a treaty on the matter. If these states feel that other states also ought to be party of such treaty because they could potentially contribute to epidemics, they could exert pressure on them to do so through normal diplomacy (including with the support of transnational pressure groups).

What is particularly disturbing in the last two quotes of Reinicke and Rosenau is the suggestion that representative democracy is not only impractical at the global level of government, but also threatened at the national level. Journalist Thomas Friedman explains that states are restrained by what he calls the "golden straightjacket" of globalization and neoliberalism.[24] In the absence of adequate global regulation, freedom of movement of capital, goods, services, and increasingly of people dramatically constrains national governments' maneuvering room for managing their economies, because national regulations that are not market friendly tend to chase capital and people away. For example, governments would hesitate to increase their taxes on capital income to balance their budget, for fear that investors would place their money elsewhere, where taxes were lower. This could potentially lead to a race to the bottom in capital taxes, which could limit governments' leverage.

It is clear that the golden straightjacket, especially the fear of capital flight, is taming governments of small- and medium-sized countries. (Big economies like the United States and the European Union enjoy a larger degree of protection because the rest of the world could hardly absorb and competitively remunerate their entire stock of capital: Their capital is less likely to flee because it has fewer places to go.) But this notion of the golden straightjacket has been overplayed. Despite what Friedman calls the "electronic herd" of financial operators moving money at light speed through the wires, capital flows can be effectively controlled with adequate international cooperation. The U.S. government could probably harness such cooperation and lead the G8 and the rest of the international community to renationalize economic management. It does not do this because the American people do not want it—nor do Europeans. (The U.S. government has led the world to control capital flows in a much more limited way, to fight money laundering and the financing of terrorism.) Globalization is indeed undermining democracy in most countries, but it is by choice of those in power at the global level of government.

Besides dismissing representative democracy as impractical at the global level of government and highlighting its shortcomings at the national level, proponents of the "governance without government" paradigm oversell what it has to offer in terms of democratic control. Having discarded elections, the elements of democracy that they emphasize are the triad of transparency, accountability, and participation.

Transparency is mostly about maximizing freedom of information (e.g., publishing the minutes of an organization's deliberative meetings). The Aarhus Convention signed by most European states is, for instance, a model commitment of governments to publish information on all kinds of environmental hazards, allowing citizens and private organizations to seek redress in court if and when governments fail to provide the information they seek.[25]

Accountability is about ensuring that organizations (governments but also businesses and civil society organizations) do all they can to achieve their stated missions and objectives. Innovations in that regard would include the World Bank's Independent Panel that deals with complaints from those affected by its projects, and the corporate so-

cial responsibility reports that many large companies now produce each
year.

Finally, participation is about giving citizens, experts, and civil society organizations the widest opportunities to give input into global
public policies. The multistakeholder processes and public-private partnerships discussed earlier are two common opportunities. The big the-
matic conferences organized by the United Nations are other consultation opportunities (e.g., the Earth Summit in Rio de Janeiro in 1992, the
Beijing World Conference on Women in 1995).[26] Participation can also
mean letting civil society organizations implement global public policies.
For example, nongovernmental organizations play an important role in
the implementation of governmental humanitarian relief programs.

Taken together, such mechanisms to foster transparency, accountability, and participation help all global actors hold each other accountable, which is the fourth tenet of the "governance without government"
paradigm. Like the paradigm itself, calls for transparency, accountability,
and participation have become very popular among civil society leaders,
international civil servants, national politicians, and even businesspeople.
For Kofi Annan, former Secretary General of the United Nations, "better
governance means greater participation coupled with accountability."[27]
(It does not necessarily mean democracy?)

In her book *The Coming Democracy*, Florini has popularized the
"governance without government" paradigm and, while acknowledging
that it is not a panacea, insists that increased transparency will make the
world a much better place.[28] While the book mentions promising initiatives, her enthusiasm for transparency is sometimes excessive, as in this
paragraph excerpted from her conclusion where she paints a picture of
the world in the year 2020:

> Most national governments are parties to the Economic Information
> Convention, negotiated in 2010. Originally promoted primarily by the
> IMF and the United States, the Economic Information Convention
> builds on IMF data dissemination standards but also includes a
> broader range of information of interest to citizens as well as investors.
> The information flows fostered by that convention have gone far to

reduce the suspicion and ignorance in which earlier debates over global economic governance were conducted.[29]

The International Monetary Fund and other intergovernmental organizations already provide a wealth of economic data, on the basis of which professional economists have debated for years over global economic policies. In the end, economics is not an ideologically neutral discipline, and I doubt that any amount of new data and transparency will ever end the right-left political divide. The adequate mechanism to settle the debate on broad economic policy directions is elections.

Transparency, accountability, and participation are certainly welcome and should be fostered by all means. But they will not resolve acute political disagreements and conflicts. They will not shift the balance of power to enable deep changes in global public policies. It is, by the way, worth noting that most authors writing on this subject limit themselves to the economic and environmental global public policy areas, and sometimes touch on human rights and disarmament. They neglect the area of international peace and security. Will Iran ever become transparent about its nuclear program? Would such transparency diffuse tension or rather precipitate war? The issue is of course not lack of transparency per se, but rather deeply rooted mistrust and disagreements about how the world should be run.

Slaughter takes a slightly different view of global governance. Although she acknowledges the importance of transnational business and civil society networks, she emphasizes the continued centrality of states and intergovernmental relations in world politics.[30] However, she points out that states are disaggregated. National government agencies, judges, and even parliamentarians reach out to their counterparts across borders to share information and solve problems. For examples, judges use precedents that occurred in other countries to solve complex cases, or police forces collaborate across borders to fight transnational crime. Such networks of national government officials can be formal or informal, and they are often set up and function in great autonomy from foreign ministries.

Cross-border collaboration of government officials is not new but it is a growing phenomenon, which is indeed interesting to take into account in analyzing world politics. But Slaughter makes the extra step of presenting her thesis in a prescriptive way. She starts by claiming, without argumentation, that "world government is both infeasible and undesirable. The size and scope of such a government presents an unavoidable and dangerous threat to individual liberty."[31] She goes on, arguing that a world order characterized by networks of national government officials is just, and that it could be improved by, among other things, increasing opportunities for citizens' participation in or interaction with them.

This argument again oversells what is on offer. Some of the networks Slaughter mentions, like the Financial Action Task Force that was created to fight money laundering by terrorists and other criminals in the aftermath of September 11, 2001, received a strong steer from the highest levels of member governments. Those networks that really do function below the radar of cabinet ministers are generally only able to solve fairly technical (even if important) problems. Networks of national government officials are no more adequate to solve big political questions than transparency of information is.

WHILE ANALYSTS AT THE center of the political spectrum do not see a need for representative democracy at the global level of government, those on the left do not have much enthusiasm for it either, although they do not reject the idea. Many left-of-center activists believe in the role of the state as a driver of development and are favorable about the idea of a global government. But they are also weary of democracy as we know it at the national level, are attracted by innovative forms of participatory democracy, and in that way are seduced by the "governance without government" paradigm.

It is undeniable that democracy is under strain. One problem has already been mentioned: the so-called golden straightjacket of globalization and neoliberalism. It can be fixed by extending democracy to the global level of government, which is what this book is about. If the world population wanted to restrain globalization to allow for stronger economic management at the national level of government, global democracy would allow for the creation of the necessary mechanisms to control capital flows.

A second problem is the influence of money in politics, which in some countries veers toward institutionalized corruption. That problem can be fixed with good laws on election financing, as testified by several countries, notably in Northern Europe. But it is of course more easily done in societies where income inequality is small to begin with; and such laws face stiff ideological opposition in the United States.

A third problem of democracy is also particularly acute in the United States: gerrymandering. As the *Economist* magazine put it: "In elections, it is said, voters choose politicians; in redistricting, it is the other way round."[32] This problem is specific to a few countries and is unfortunately persistent.

The fourth problem that most if not all democratic societies face is the depoliticization of large segments of their populations, which manifests itself by either low participation rates at elections or high scores for populist and sectarian parties. This last problem is the most disturbing one because it is both widespread and hard to address. Popular mobilization and issue campaigning by civil society organizations are ways to reengage people disaffected by the formal political system. Efforts to increase transparency, accountability, and most of all participation at the global level of government are very important to keep democracy alive and thriving, and can complement and indeed build on initiatives to increase citizen activism at the local level.

Buoyant citizen participation in political processes is an absolutely necessary component of democracy. But it is a complement, not a substitute, for the electoral process. A few thinkers advocate radical forms of participatory democracy.[33] In my opinion, though, none has yet come up with an alternative to representative democracy that is both legitimate and practical. Activists who fought against authoritarian regimes at the national level of government know the value of representative democracy better than Florida or Ohio voters. They would gain by putting global representative democracy on the agenda, alongside continued work on transparency, accountability, and participation.

IN SUM, GOVERNANCE WITHOUT government means little more than government without democracy. Neither Rosenau, nor I, nor anyone else has yet imagined a mechanism to give power to the people that is as good as representative democracy with equal universal suffrage and the majority rule. In fairness to Rosenau, he has himself always presented the "governance without government" paradigm as a description, not a prescription. Although enthusiastic about the descriptive power of his theory, he admits that the atomization of power is a poor substitute for democracy as we know it: "It may well leave the reader, like the author, feeling let down, as if it ought to be possible to write an upbeat final chapter of this story of democratic development in a disaggregated and fragmenting global system of governance."[34] Rather than preserving the paradigm and succumbing to pessimism about the future of representative democracy that it entails, I personally prefer to try harder to find practical ways to extend some elements of democracy as we know it at the national level to the global level of government. This choice is consistent with the third paradigm—besides world federalism and "governance without government"—that has emerged to analyze the global village.

This third paradigm, "cosmopolitan democracy," was articulated by political theorist David Held.[35] It seeks to "specify principles and institutional arrangements for making accountable those sites and forms of power which presently operate beyond the scope of democratic control" and to "integrate and limit the functions of existing states with new institutions based on world citizenship."[36]

Cosmopolitan democracy can be described as a synthesis of world federalism and "governance without government." Like world federalism, cosmopolitan democracy duly recognizes the importance of states and international institutions in the global village. But it notes that the boundary between the two becomes increasingly blurred as international institutions gain autonomy and acquire attributes of states. Like the "governance without government" paradigm, cosmopolitan democracy also recognizes the important roles of private actors in the global village, and predicts that the institutional architecture of the global village will evolve and increase in complexity—in contrast with the static and neat world government dreamed by world federalists. The paradigm also combines representative notions of democracy with new forms of participation, including direct participation of citizen groups in international institutions.

According to the cosmopolitan democracy paradigm, the world

might come to increasingly resemble medieval Europe—before the notion of the sovereign state took root thanks to the 1648 Treaties of Westphalia—where a hierarchy of local, state, national, and supranational public authorities would share sovereignty over particular territories just as barons, earls, princes, and kings or emperors used to do; where the Universal Declaration of Human Rights and civil society organizations would play the respective roles of the Bible (the unifying moral code) and the clergy (the defenders of that moral code); and where multinational businesses would be equivalent to the medieval guilds of merchants claiming chartered rights from their lords.

Cosmopolitan democracy is a prescriptive paradigm, but unlike world federalism it is rooted in realities we can already observe. To better understand the cosmopolitan democratic world that is now unfolding, I now propose to rejuvenate some old concepts, including federalism and confederalism, sovereignty, subsidiarity and competences, functionalism and regionalism. In the remaining chapters of Part I, I will seek to narrow the definitions of these concepts down to their essence. That will allow me to combine these concepts in multiple ways in Part III, creating institutions that are hybrids between states and intergovernmental organizations. Such institutional innovations stand in sharp contrast to Glossop's binary view of institutions, pitting world government against intergovernmental organizations. These innovations will also allow thinking about the institutional architecture of the global village in dynamic terms, and sketch how democracy as we know it at the national level could progressively develop at the global level of government.

4

Federalism and Confederalism

FOR MOST STATES, WORLD federalism is already a reality. They share power with some intergovernmental organizations like the World Trade Organization in a way similar to the way Kansas shares power with the United States of America. To explain this provocative proposition, I propose a fresh definition of the concepts of federalism and confederalism that allows understanding better the nature of intergovernmental organizations and how they could evolve toward global democracy.

The essence of the distinction between federations and confederations lies in the way their member-states make decisions. I will distinguish three decision-making rules: weak confederalism, strong confederalism, and federalism. The statutes of most intergovernmental organizations involve more than one of these rules, depending on the type of decisions to be made.

In weak confederations, member-states have an opt-out right but no veto right over decisions. An opt-out right is the right for a member-state not to implement decisions of a given intergovernmental organization. A veto right is the right for a member-state to block decisions proposed within an intergovernmental organization. In weak confederations, member-states can thus not be forced to comply with a given global public policy, but they are also unable to prevent others from adopting it for themselves.

Weak confederalism is the most common decision-making rule within intergovernmental organizations. For example, treaties adopted in the framework of the United Nations, such as the Framework Convention on Climate Change or the treaty that instituted the International Criminal Court, are usually developed along the following process. The United Nations General Assembly convenes a commission to negotiate the treaty. Once an agreement emerges among a critical mass of member-states, the treaty is finalized at a conference of member-states and becomes opened for ratification. Ratification is done by each member-state individually according to its own constitution, usually by a vote in parliament. Member-states do not have any legal obligation to ratify treaties, although they may face political pressure from other member-states to do so. The treaty then comes into force when a critical mass of member-states has ratified it, and it applies only to those states that have ratified it. Most treaties are never ratified by all member-states of the United Nations. Some treaties allow national parliaments to add reservations when they ratify the treaty, which means that the same treaty may not impose exactly the same obligations on all signatories. Finally, once ratified, treaties must still be translated into national laws, because treaties themselves represent obligations of states toward each other, but not toward their citizens. There is no general rule determining how large the critical mass of ratifying member-states must be in order for a treaty to come into force. It can be less than half the total number of states that are members of the United Nations. But there is little point in adopting a treaty at the United Nations if only few nations want it. (In that case, it would make more sense to adopt the treaty within a smaller club of states, such as a regional intergovernmental organization, or even within a new organization created for the purpose of the treaty.)

Resolutions adopted by the United Nations General Assembly or its commissions like the Human Rights Council are also subject to opt-out rights, since they are not legally binding. (Some legal scholars argue that they are legally binding when adopted repeatedly by a very large majority of states.)[37] Rather, they impose some moral pressure on states to comply with generally agreed custom, and otherwise serve as barometers of where the international community stands on specific issues, a little like opinion polls.

Other forms of opt-out rights are norms or standards, and special funds. Intergovernmental organizations often set norms or standards that do not have legal status, and with which member-states may therefore comply at their entire discretion, although they may face strong economic or other incentives to comply with them (which is the case for some norms set by the International Monetary Fund that influence access to financial markets, for example). As to special funds, they finance a large share of the United Nations' peacekeeping and aid programs and are funded by voluntary contributions of member-states instead of by the mandatory contributions that states must pay in virtue of their membership. That contributions are voluntary means that member-states can opt out of any contribution greater than they are ready to pay.

Strong confederations are the opposite of weak confederations. Member-states of strong confederations have veto rights but no opt-out rights. Hence they may prevent a global public policy from being adopted, but once adopted, they must comply with it. The United Nations Security Council is therefore a strong confederation from the perspective of its five permanent members, which are entitled to a veto right. Its resolutions are indeed legally binding—so there is no opt-out right. The most important decisions of the European Union, including the budget, treaty amendments, admission of new members, and more, are also adopted according to strong confederalism.

Finally, in federations, member-states have neither veto nor opt-out rights. In other words, they may be forced to implement decisions made by other member-states but with which they disagree. Decisions in federations are typically made by majority vote, with a number of variations. The majority may mean either a simple majority (at least 50 percent of the votes) or a supermajority (such as at least two-thirds or three-quarters of the votes), the latter being generally preferred for important decisions. Each member-state may get either one vote or a number of votes roughly proportional to its population (like in the European Union) or its financial contribution to the organization (like in the International Monetary Fund and the World Bank, in which the financial contributions are themselves set as a rough proportion of each state's importance in international trade and finance).

The Security Council is a federation from the perspective of all states except its five permanent members: Other states may not veto its decisions but must comply with them. The International Monetary Fund and the World Bank are federations for all their member-states except the United States, which has sufficient votes to veto decisions requiring supermajorities. The European Union is also a federation for most decisions that it makes. The statutes of many other intergovernmental organizations also allow for majority voting for certain kinds of binding decisions, usually low-stake ones such as approving their administrative budgets. However, they often specify that consensus ought to be sought before taking a vote, and, in practice, consensus or strong confederalism does prevail most of the time.

The advantage of weak confederalism is its flexibility. Since no member-state can prevent others from taking initiatives, it accommodates a large number of members with diverse interests and values. Its disadvantage is the lack of discipline. No state can ever be forced to implement decisions that it does not like. Not surprisingly, the advantages and disadvantages of strong confederalism are the opposite. It is very inflexible, as unanimity is required for every decision. But it is also very cohesive, as decisions can be enforced in all member-states. It is therefore best suited to unions among a small number of states that share a common sense of purpose. Finally, federalism combines the advantages of both forms of confederalism, but it supposes that member-states accept to implement decisions that they might not endorse. Federations therefore require a higher degree of trust and solidarity among their member-states, or what I called a stronger political community.

This classification is important to assess voting rights within intergovernmental organizations. In weak confederations, voting rights do not matter much since member-states that are outvoted can exercise their opt-out right anyway. By contrast, the distribution of votes among member-states is very important in federations, as states with fewer votes are more likely to be outvoted and hence be forced to implement decisions with which they disagree. (In strong confederations, member-states always have equal voting power: Each can block any decision.)

Note that one should not confuse an opt-out right with a secession right. The secession right is the right for a state to quit an intergovernmental organization or not to join it in the first place, and hence to free itself from any obligations and rights. It exists in all intergovernmental organizations, with the notable exception of the Security Council when it acts under Chapter VII of the United Nations Charter. (Chapter VII gives the Security Council authority to authorize the use of force to restore international peace.) Even if some states chose to quit the United Nations, they would still be bound by the Security Council's resolutions aiming at enforcing peace.

Now that these definitions are established, it is important to distinguish the decision-making rules specified in intergovernmental organizations' statutes from both their decision-making practice and the power structure that underpins them. I have already mentioned that where federalism exists in statutes, the practice is often that of strong confederalism. (Two important exceptions in that regard are the Security Council and the European Union, where a practice of votes does exist and states that lose a vote do accept the majority decision—or face the consequences of sanctions.)

As to the underlying power structure, the United States has the capacity to veto all decisions in the key intergovernmental organizations, and almost all decisions in all other organizations. It has formal veto rights in the most important bodies: the Security Council and, for decisions requiring supermajorities, the International Monetary Fund and the World Bank. It also has an informal veto capacity in the fourth key organization, the World Trade Organization, because the American market's size in world trade is such that any trade agreement that would not be implemented by the United States would be unworkable in the rest of the world. The economic and military importance of the United States is actually such that its participation is critical to the success of any global public policy. That gives the United States an informal veto capacity in most global public policy decisions. However, some initiatives that have strong European support are sometimes adopted by intergovernmental organizations in the face of American opposition, such as the Kyoto Protocol of the Framework Convention on Climate Change, the Rome Statutes of the International Criminal Court, and a number of other human rights treaties. As all these initiatives are adopted according to weak confederalism, the United States has an opt-out right and does not hesitate to exercise it. In sum, the United States does not belong to any federation; it is never forced to adopt global public policies that it does not endorse.

The European Union's influence or that of its member-states in intergovernmental organizations is also tremendous. Europeans have veto capacity for virtually all decisions in all of the organizations. Two European Union members have veto rights in the Security Council, and European Union member-states collectively have a very high share of votes at the International Monetary Fund and the World Bank (though it falls short of a simple majority, it definitely provides vast and disproportional influence to Europeans). As in the case of the United States, trade agreements would not be viable without the European Union's endorsement. Most other initiatives would also be severely undermined by a lack of European support. Moreover, European Union member-states benefit from a large voting block in organizations where decisions are taken by the "one state, one vote" voting rule. Its twenty-seven members are not obliged to vote as a block in most intergovernmental organizations, but they often do so because their positions are well aligned on global public policy issues (the war against Iraq started in 2003 being an exception). European positions are also often more suitable to the rest of the world than those of the United States. As a result, I cannot think of any significant global public policy set by intergovernmental organizations that Europeans have not endorsed. Not only do Europeans not belong to any global federation, but they also seldom have to exercise their opt-out rights in the weak confederations to which they belong.

When the positions of the United States and the Europeans are aligned on a given global public policy issue, their combined veto power is absolute in all intergovernmental organizations. And since they share many values and interests compared to the rest of the world, due to their shared cultural heritage and stage of economic development, their positions are often aligned. The United States definitely has much more influence than the Europeans on security issues, thanks to its unmatched military capacity. (And that military power also allows the United States to leverage the support of other states on many issues not directly related to security.) On other issues, such as trade or environmental protection, both superpowers negotiate more or less as equals.

When they fail to agree, the United States and the Europeans both have the power to undermine each other, though they often cannot entirely block each other's actions. As I have noted, the Europeans can sometimes push their preferred policies through weak confederations. But the United States can exercise its opt-out right, which always undermines the implementation of these policies (the Kyoto Protocol and the International Criminal Court being good examples in that regard). On the other hand, the United States does not hesitate to act entirely outside of the framework of intergovernmental organizations, sometimes even in contravention of international law as was the case with the invasion of Iraq. But the lack of legitimacy of the United States' unilateral actions also undermines their effectiveness to some degree, as the difficulties encountered by the United States in stamping out the insurrection and reconstructing Iraq demonstrate, for example.

Besides the United States and the Europeans, a few other states have the capacity to veto decisions in certain intergovernmental organizations. China and Russia have formal veto rights in the Security Council, which is a significant privilege that they do exercise (rarely in public sessions of the Security Council but often in private negotiations that happen beforehand and that persuade the other Security Council members not to push for a formal vote). Japan benefits, in the same way as the United States and Europe do, from an informal veto capacity at the World Trade Organization and in intergovernmental organizations regulating international finance. Besides these three exceptions, it is probably fair to say that no single state benefits from a veto capacity in any intergovernmental organizations, although some big powers like Australia, Brazil, Canada, China, India, and Russia can exert considerable influence in many organizations.

For states other than the United States and the European Union member-states, veto capacity in intergovernmental organizations is thus exceptional. From the perspective of most states, intergovernmental organizations are either weak confederations or federations, even when the decision-making practice is consensus.

Besides the exceptions noted above, states accept the veil of consensus and do not veto decisions because they know that their formal vetoes could be circumvented. That is certainly true when the relevant intergovernmental organization's statutes allow for majority voting in case consensus cannot be found (that is, when federalism is statutorily allowed as a last resort). But it is also generally true when strong confederalism must be legally strictly observed. The European Union and the United States can always circumvent the threat of vetoes by one or a few other states in two ways. They can threaten to bypass the intergovernmental organization in which the contested global public policy is negotiated, and push for that policy to be adopted in another forum that does not include the dissenting states—possibly a new intergovernmental organization created for that purpose. Alternatively, they can put tremendous pressure on the vetoing states through off-the-table carrots and sticks, that is, through positive and negative incentives unrelated to the decision or intergovernmental organization at hand. As a result, and the exceptions noted above notwithstanding, states can exercise their formal veto right in strong confederations only when they manage to muster large coalitions. They do not have veto capacity individually.

Even that collective veto capacity is of limited value. If a coalition of small and medium-sized countries confronts the European Union or the United States, the result is an impasse, since these two entities have a veto capacity of their own. Given that the European Union and the United States suffer less from the status quo than other states on most issues, and have more maneuvering room for generating global public policies outside of the framework of intergovernmental organizations, they have the upper hand to negotiate any agreements to break deadlocks. The budgets of United Nations aid agencies serve as a clear example of this. A coalition of poor countries could break the tradition of consensus and vote as a block against budget proposals shaped largely by rich countries. But the latter, even though they would be in the minority as far as voting power is concerned, could simply opt out of resourcing the special funds on which these agencies depend, which would be devastating for the poor countries' coalition. I will provide further illustrations of such situations in Part III.

All states can of course generate global public policies outside of the framework of intergovernmental organizations, either through regional organizations or by acting unilaterally or bilaterally. (Remember that I defined global public policies as "public policies that affect most if not all people—or specified categories of people—throughout the world, whether they emanate from national or local governments, intergovernmental organizations, or even from the private sector.") But the global repercussions of these policies will typically be limited by the economic, military, or other forms of power of the states that initiate them. Intergovernmental organizations do have both legal and moral authority that significantly augment the reach of global public policies. Acting through intergovernmental organizations also allows leveraging resources from other member-states.

In sum, although their statutes allow for a variety of decision-making rules and despite a widespread decision-making practice of consensus, intergovernmental organizations are either weak or strong confederations from the perspective of the United States and the European Union member-states, but they are either weak confederations or federations from the point of view of all other states (with a few exceptions for specific states in specific intergovernmental organizations). In that sense, the global village is characterized by apartheid, with different classes of nations enjoying different political rights, and with a minority of people dominating the majority. The United States and the Europeans, representing only a little more than 10 percent of the world's population, clearly run intergovernmental organizations, even if coalitions of other states may force them to compromise.

Furthermore, the decision-making rules have not been randomly assigned across intergovernmental organizations. For the issues that matter most to the United States and the European Union, namely security and international trade and finance, the dominant rule is strong confederalism for the United States and the Europeans and federalism for the rest of the world. This is reflected in the statutes of the Security Council, International Monetary Fund, and World Bank. Federalism allows the United States and the Europeans to impose greater discipline in the implementation of global public policies that matter to them. For the other issues, such as poverty alleviation and environmental protection, the dominant decision-making rule is weak confederalism for all states, which allows the United States and the Europeans to opt out of global public policies and therefore neglect their responsibilities. This is not unlike pre-1994 South Africa, where the white regime created puppet states called Bantustans, where the bulk of the black population lived. The Bantustans were responsible for the welfare of their residents, which was a way for the South African state to discharge its responsibility to care for its black citizens. On the other hand, the whites retained exclusive control not only over the territories not attributed to Bantustans, but also over security issues and the relationship between the South African state and the Bantustans.

My claim that most states have no choice but to accept public policies decided by key intergovernmental organizations suggests that their sovereignty is limited. Demystifying the concept of sovereignty, like that of federalism, is also useful for understanding global democracy.

5

Sovereignty

"SOVEREIGNTY" IS A VERY loaded word, and the loss of sovereignty is often used by nationalists to decry initiatives of the international community. A loss of sovereignty is regarded as a loss of control over the national fate. They forget to say that nations rarely surrender control over their destinies unilaterally, and that when others also accept the obligations of new treaties, it can make everyone better off. Indeed, globalization itself is nothing but a growing interdependence that limits the state's control over the national fate, whether it is managed by strong or weak international institutions. I am going to unpack the concept of sovereignty to show that it is, in the end, not very relevant to global democracy.

It may be useful to start by noting what sovereignty is not. Sovereignty is usually associated with the following features, even though none of them are exclusive or necessary attributes of sovereign states:

- *Printing money*: Not all sovereign states print their own money, such as some dollarized countries in Latin America. On the other hand, some nonsovereign entities do, such as the West African Economic and Monetary Union.
- *Raising taxes*: Some intergovernmental organizations such as customs unions have some tax power, even though they delegate the actual collection of taxes to lower levels of government. Most nonsovereign local governments have some taxation power, too.

On the other hand, some small sovereign states raise very little tax revenue.

- *Maintaining an army*: Iceland and Costa Rica do not have an army, but they are sovereign states. On the other hand, the United Nations would not become sovereign were it to raise a small standing force of mercenary peacekeepers.
- *Parliament*: Most local governments have directly elected parliaments, so parliaments cannot be an exclusive attribute of sovereignty. The European Union also has a directly elected parliament, and several other intergovernmental organizations such as the Council of Europe have assemblies composed of parliamentarians of their member-states. On the other hand, the Vatican is a sovereign state without parliament.
- *Constitution*: The Swiss cantons and the states of the United States of America have constitutions without being sovereign in regard of international law. Constitutions are commonly regarded as conferring "popular sovereignty" because they usually assert that all powers of the state ultimately emanate from the people. In fact, the line separating treaties establishing intergovernmental organizations such as the European Union and constitutions of federal states such as the United States of America can be very thin. The difference ultimately rests upon the identity of the signatories: Treaties are signed by representatives of the federated entities while constitutions are signed by individual members of constitutional conventions. (The signed but not ratified "constitution" of the European Union was really a treaty in that regard, although it was originally drafted by a constitutional convention.) This distinction has little significance beyond a sentimental one. Constitutional conventions are not periodically recalled to confirm the will of the people to be ruled by a particular form of government, and in many cases they were not even directly elected by all the people in the first place. By contrast, treaties transferring competences to intergovernmental organizations are sometimes subject to referendum and, in democracies, always signed by elected officials.
- *National symbols*: Flags, anthems, and holidays are obviously not what constitute sovereignty, and indeed any sport club, religious

congregation, or ethnic group can create those elements as well. In some countries, the sovereign state is by far the primary source of personal identity. For example, Koreans tend to identify themselves as Koreans above all else. But in other countries, identities are shaped by multiple categories: race, religion, language, and so on. I have also shown that many people have shared allegiances between their local, national, and supranational governments.

IF NOT ANY OF these elements, what constitutes sovereignty? The definition of sovereignty used by scholars of international affairs goes back to the notion of control over the national destiny. International lawyers have a very pragmatic way of assessing whether a particular political entity ruling over a specific territory is sovereign. They simply observe whether it is recognized as such by the international community (that is, by most if not all other sovereign states). Besides the United Nations' 192 member-states plus the Holy See, which is only observer, two additional territories are generally recognized as sovereign states: the Cooks Islands and Niue (both of them islands in the Pacific Ocean). A few problematic territories, including Palestine, may earn sovereignty in the future.[38]

States thus derive their sovereignty from control over their foreign policy in general, and from the recognition by other states of their authority to sign treaties and send representatives to intergovernmental organizations in particular. The recognition of sovereignty is largely based on an observation of reality—does a certain political entity have an independent foreign policy or not?—but it is ultimately a political decision. Taiwan, for instance, does have an independent foreign policy but is not generally considered a sovereign state because China has persuaded most states not to recognize it as such. Taiwan is not a member of the United Nations nor of most other major intergovernmental organizations, although it seeks to align itself with their policies and to influence them through bilateral diplomacy, and it is otherwise treated much as any sovereign state.

In almost every state, foreign policy has been an exclusive prerogative of the national level of government, because allowing local governments to pass conflicting treaties with foreign states may jeopardize smooth relationships among them or between them and the national government.

But it does not need to be that way. Foreign policy could be shared in federal states, provided that the respective competences of the federation and its federated entities are clearly defined. ("Competences" are the policy areas in which the federation and its member-states can respectively legislate.)

Belgium is the federal state that has gone the furthest in devolving foreign policy to its federated entities. Since 1993, the Belgian federated entities may sign treaties in the public policy areas over which they are competent on their own territories, such as education and culture. However, because it is a novelty, the international community has so far been reluctant to recognize their sovereignty in those policy areas and to formally grant them seats in intergovernmental organizations. As a result, when the Belgian federated entities settle international treaties, their representatives add footnotes below their signatures explaining that they are entitled to do so by the Belgian constitution, and that the Belgian state endorses full responsibility for their commitments.[39] The federated entities of Germany and Switzerland also have limited foreign policy competences. By contrast, in 2000 the U.S. Supreme Court struck down the Myanmar boycott law, by which the Commonwealth of Massachusetts was asserting its voice on foreign policy. In sum, entities of federal states have thus far not been considered sovereign, but this is a convention reflecting current practice, not a necessity. If more federal states were to go the Belgian way, the international community would have to put up with the notion that their federated entities share sovereignty.

Pragmatism also prevails to assess the status of intergovernmental organizations, regardless of their decision-making rules (weak or strong confederations or federations). They are not recognized as sovereign. Nevertheless, the European Union is considered as equal to sovereign states as far as international trade law is concerned, because its twenty-seven member-states have decided to send a single person to negotiate trade agreements. The European Union is a full member of the World Trade Organization, as well as of the Food and Agriculture Organization, because it also runs the agricultural policy of its member-states. On the other hand, the International Labor Organization has been touchier, deciding to stick with the principle of admitting only states, such that the European Union is not a member despite its competences in labor policy.

The fifteen European governments are therefore obliged to organize preparatory meetings in order to come up with a common position before the International Labor Organization's plenary sessions. Again, if more intergovernmental organizations were to follow the European Union's precedent, the international community would probably pragmatically start recognizing their sovereignty.

Sovereignty can be an important asset in international relations. Tibet's loss of sovereignty after its invasion by China in 1950 has had dramatic consequences for its population. The prospect of sovereignty for Palestine could also prove important for Palestinians. (Yet the opposite examples of Tibet and Taiwan remind us that the international community's recognition of a political entity's sovereignty and its commitment to defend that entity's territory are different things: The international community did not protect sovereign Tibet in 1950, but the United States is committed to defending nonsovereign Taiwan today.)

However, for the purpose of studying the relationships between local governments, states, and intergovernmental organizations, sovereignty is not a very meaningful concept. Lack of sovereignty can be compensated by a footnote below a signature, as in the case of the Belgian federated entities, or by preparatory meetings in intergovernmental organizations, as in the European Union case, or even by a good dose of hypocrisy, as in the case of Taiwan (which was pragmatically admitted at the World Trade Organization in 2003 under the name "SEPARATE CUSTOMS TERRITORY OF TAIWAN, PENGHU, KINMEN AND MATSU"—lest anyone think it is a sovereign state).

The really relevant questions to assess the relative power of intergovernmental organizations and their member-states, or of federal states and their federated entities, are the following: Do member-states have either a veto or opt-out right for all or some categories of decisions? If neither, what is the distribution of votes among them? Do they keep the right to secede? Which policy areas are assigned to which level of government? And which level of government has "competence over competence," that is, which level of government can change the distribution of competences among the various levels of government?

All of these questions do influence the degree to which states are able to control their destiny. However, absolute control no longer exists in the era of globalization. Even the United States accepts rules it does not like, such as opening the textile industry to foreign competition, in exchange for similar concessions by its trading partners. The loss of sovereignty (in the sense of absolute control over the national fate) may appear small when it takes the form of discrete quid pro quo agreements. It is more striking when a large number of quid pro quo agreements are bundled together in the form of marathon negotiation rounds at the World Trade Organization, for instance. And it may appear even more alarming when it takes the form of joining a federal intergovernmental organization, where decisions are taken by majority vote instead of unanimity. Yet even federalism is a quid pro quo of a higher order: Instead of being willing to cut my import tariff on sugar in exchange for you cutting your tariff on computer software, federalism means that we both are willing to set trade rules by majority vote. Sometimes I will win the vote, sometimes you will. In either case, control over the national fate is preserved in the sense that decisions have been freely devolved to a certain decision-making forum and can be taken back.

The notion of sovereignty itself is thus not very useful to a discussion of global democracy. The concept of federalism and that of competence (or authority to make public policy in specific policy areas) of each level of government are more important. I now turn to the latter.

6

Competences and Subsidiarity

ONCE THE CONCEPTS OF government, sovereignty, federation, and confederation are disentangled, it becomes easier to think of government as a multilayered body. As sovereignty is not a very meaningful concept to assess the nature or relative power of various levels of government, intergovernmental organizations can then be conceived of as extra layers of government in the same way local governments are—since local governments are not sovereign either. Residents of most territories are then governed by six or seven levels of government:

1. Town or city
2. County
3. State
4. National or federal government
5. Subregional intergovernmental organizations (e.g., North American Free Trade Area, North Atlantic Treaty Organization)
6. Regional intergovernmental organizations (e.g., Organization of American States)
7. Global intergovernmental organizations (e.g., United Nations)

For unitary states, the national level is by far the most important one, and the third level (equivalent to states of the United States of America) does not exist. In federal states, the third and fourth levels share most competences. In federal states belonging to the European Union (e.g.,

Belgium, Germany, Spain), levels 3, 4, and 5 share most competences, the European Union being at level 5.

I define the concept of competence as the authority of making public policies in a particular policy area, whether such policies take the form of laws, treaties and nonbinding resolutions, standards and norms, or public expenditure programs. I also consider that weak confederations have competences even if they cannot enforce their public policies. For instance, the United Nations Human Rights Council does not have the means to enforce its recommendations but is nevertheless competent for human rights issues.

Although circumstances vary country by country, it is fair to say that many competences have been devolved from the national level to both lower and higher levels of government over the past few decades. The globalization phenomenon has led to a strengthening of global intergovernmental organizations like the World Trade Organization, whose competences have become considerable. Many states have also devolved competences to either state or local governments.

All seven levels of government are competent for some aspects of most public policy areas—or conversely, most if not all public policy areas are usually partitioned among several levels of government. Even defense policy, which is commonly regarded as the quintessential prerogative of national governments, is sometimes split among several levels of government. Besides the peacekeeping role played by the United Nations and level-6 intergovernmental organizations such as the African Union, small member-states of the North Atlantic Treaty Organization (NATO), for example, do not have an independent defense capacity. While they have kept human resources management and equipment procurement at level 4, they have devolved other essential defense functions to level 5 (that is, to NATO or its bigger member-states), including nuclear deterrence, intelligence, communication and logistical infrastructure, contingency planning, and research and development of new weapons.

The different functions of government may also be split among different levels of government for a given legislation or expenditure program. For example, funds for a particular social program may be raised at one level of government and spent at another, under regulations set by a third level.

THE NOTION OF MULTILAYERED government obviously raises the question of what should determine such distribution of competences among the various levels of government. The principle of subsidiarity is usually invoked to answer that question. It holds that public policy decisions ought to be made at the lowest efficient level of government. In other words, higher levels of government should be called upon only to the extent that there are compelling efficiency gains in transferring policy making to them. For example, water management should rationally be assigned to all levels of government, depending on which territories are contiguous to any given water resource: Ponds are best managed at the first level of government and oceans at the seventh.

However, the subsidiarity principle is of little use. Water management is an exception. Most competences do not have a logical or uncontroversial level of government to be assigned to. Since assigning a competence at a higher level of government typically reduces the diversity of public policies, there is always a tension between efficiency and respect for local preferences. For example, education is a competence of the states in the United States of America, and states' rights advocates want it to stay that way to respect diversity. However, the federal budget for education is creeping up because some regard federal funds as an efficient incentive for states to raise educational standards.

Moreover, disagreements over the trade-off between efficiency and diversity of preferences are not the only thing that makes the subsidiarity principle of little use. The degree of solidarity among federated entities of a federal state, or among member-states of an intergovernmental organization, is probably a bigger determinant of the assignment of competences among levels of government. Defense policy is a case in point. The most efficient level of government for defense policy is the seventh: If there were only one global army, there would not be any wars. But people are typically not ready to die to protect nationals of any other states, thus defense alliances develop less on the basis of efficiency than on grounds of solidarity.

Ultimately, what ought to determine the distribution of competences among the different levels of government is, therefore, the will of the people. Assigning a competence within a multilayered government is equivalent to determining whether an issue belongs to the public interest, and therefore could be legislated on, or must be considered as a private matter that government should not touch. From marijuana consumption to adultery, all societies struggle with the boundaries between public interest and private domain. Any issue, even the most private one, may potentially be legislated on if a majority of legislators want it, within the limits of the constitution and of any bill of rights attached to it—but then the constitution or bill of rights may itself be amended (the proposed ban on gay marriage in the United States being an example). In most states, amending the constitution requires either a supermajority vote in parliament (e.g., two-thirds or three-fourths) or a referendum (itself requiring either a simple majority or supermajority) or both. That is because the very legitimacy of the legislative body is at stake. When it comes to tinkering with the boundaries between public interest and private domain through constitutional amendments, citizens need to be protected from the risk of their parliament extending the public interest limitlessly and awarding itself the power to rule every aspect of human life, hence the supermajorities and referendums. But within the utmost boundaries of the public interest set by a state's constitution, parliament can legislate by single majority.

Moving a competence to a higher level of government is equivalent to deciding that it belongs to the public interest not only of a country, but also of a region or of the whole humanity. Just as parliaments may tinker with their own states' constitutions, any groups of parliaments already are and should continue to be able to ratify new treaties to modify the competences of particular intergovernmental organizations. Such transfers of competences between states and intergovernmental organizations should be decided by supermajorities of member-states for the same reason as amendments to national constitutions should be decided by supermajorities of citizens. At this time, changing the competence of any intergovernmental organization requires unanimous consent of its member-states.

Among the seven levels of government, level 4 has indeed almost a monopoly on "competence over competence," the prerogative of assigning competences among various levels of government. National governments can devolve competences both upward to intergovernmental organizations by signing treaties, and downward to local government by amending their constitutions. In many federal states, however, the legislative authority to transfer competences is shared between level 3 and level 4. In the United States, for example, amending the federal constitution requires both a vote by Congress and ratification by three quarters of the states. Likewise, the German federal government would not be able to devolve the competences of its federated entities, such as education policy, to the European Union without the consent of these federated entities.

In the future, one could envision partial transfers of the competence over competence to any of the seven levels of government, which would definitely represent a significant shift in the balance of power between national governments and intergovernmental organizations. For example, the European Union member-states may at some point in the future agree that it makes more sense for them to adopt amendments to European Union treaties with a supermajority rule falling short of unanimity (e.g., amendments to the European treaties would be passed if ratified by all member-states except one or two). The recent debacle over ratification of the European Union constitution has certainly put off such a prospect. But it has also revealed the need to consider such reform for intergovernmental organizations seeking very close integration while significantly expanding membership, which makes the unanimity rule unwieldy. In the long term, as the global community solidifies, sharing the competence over competence may become necessary to the development of global democracy.

But sharing the competence over competence should remain voluntary. As is the case for other transfers of competences today, states should retain the right to take it back by renouncing the relevant treaty or seceding from the relevant intergovernmental organization. The secession right could itself be put into question at some distant point in the future, but I am not sure whether that would ever be desirable, and I would certainly not advocate curtailing it within my lifetime. Critics would argue that global democracy is an oxymoron, as democracy requires checks and balances that themselves require a variety of competing institutions. That argument has a lot of merit, and I believe that the right of states to secede from intergovernmental organizations is global democracy's equivalent to the right of citizens to "vote with their feet" by emigrating to other states: It is the ultimate check to excessive government power.

For example, speaking of voting with one's feet, people from poor countries could argue that it is nonsense for the Universal Declaration of Human Rights to assert that emigration is a human right but immigration is not, that they have the right to leave their countries but not necessarily the right to enter other countries. They could press for treaties transferring some competences on migration policy to an intergovernmental organization. But states that fear excessive immigration flows should keep the right not to join such treaties. That right is currently a fundamental freedom of nations, equivalent to fundamental individual freedoms protected by constitutional bills of rights. Denying it—assuming it were possible to impose a treaty on powerful countries—would be inconsistent with the idea of liberal democracy. I am personally in favor of greater individual migration freedom, but I accept that it would develop only with the consent of host countries.

Ultimately, the global public interest is what national legislatures collectively decide it to be through treaties. The global public interest is therefore multiform, as a large number of treaties among different subsets of states, overlapping to various degrees, simultaneously define different public policy areas as areas of common interest. This multiform character of the global public interest leads me to discuss two last concepts: functionalism and regionalism.

7

Functionalism and Regionalism

O NE DIFFERENCE BETWEEN THE national and global levels of government is that national governments have a clear center, the president or prime minister with his or her cabinet as well as the parliament, while intergovernmental organizations appear like a collection of disconnected and autonomous bodies that are therefore hard to conceive of as "a" government. In reality, the latter are not so disconnected, as their constituents are by and large the same set of member-states, with the same power relations among them. But the multiplicity of organizations allows for faster development of the global village's institutional architecture. The last two concepts that need to be understood to appreciate how global democracy could emerge are thus functionalism and regionalism.

Functionalism refers to government by agencies that are specialized in particular public policy areas. The International Monetary Fund and the United Nations Educational, Scientific, and Cultural Organization (UNESCO) are specialized intergovernmental organizations dealing with, respectively, international finance and international cooperation in the areas of education, science, and culture. By contrast, the United Nations is a general organization, like national governments, dealing with all public policy areas. Both general and functional organizations can be either confederations or federations.

Functionalism is by no means unique to the global level of government. National and local governments consist of line ministries and departments that are under direct control of the executive branch, but also of a series of agencies that are more or less autonomous yet can wield substantial power, such as central banks. Many of these agencies have semiprivate status. They often involve private actors, such as professional associations, in decision making or policy implementation. In some rare cases, such as school boards in the United States, specialized agencies are even run by directly elected officials, which further emphasizes their autonomy vis-à-vis the central administration of their level of government.

Regionalism is a self-explanatory concept. As suggested when I presented the idea of multilayered government, intergovernmental organizations can be either regional or global, the latter meaning that their memberships span several continents. In turn, both types of organizations can be either selective, like the European Union that has stringent admission criteria, or universal, like the United Nations that has admission criteria so lax that any sovereign state that applies for membership is admitted.

Functionalism and regionalism are ways to introduce flexibility in the global village in the numerous cases where people of different states disagree on the adequate distribution of competences among the various levels of government. Functionalism allows for deeper international cooperation in some public policy areas, and regionalism for deeper cooperation within some groups of countries. The European Union, a regional organization, is definitely a test case for the development of global democracy. The World Trade Organization, a functional organization, similarly represents a leading experience for global organizations, as I will discuss in depth in Part III.

THE LAST FEW CHAPTERS have been fairly technical. My purpose has been to show that the institutional architecture of the global village is more complex than one would think, and that its complexity could yet increase just by developing some of the institutional oddities that already exist. In Part II and Part III, I will come back to the battery of concepts that I have presented here, and show how these concepts help us think about liberal representative democracy at the global level of government.

But before presenting global democracy in detail, I will now explain why we need it, or why the alternative approaches to foreign policy making fail to build a better world for all.

IN PART II, I POSITION global democracy by contrasting it with the four other approaches to foreign policy that are generally recognized by analysts of international affairs: benevolent imperialism, nationalism, multilateralism, and localism. I structure each of these chapters in a similar way, by (1) defining the foreign policy approach, (2) identifying its proponents, (3) explaining how it conceives the role of international institutions and how it relates to the concept of global democracy, (4) presenting a broad critique of it, and (5) applying that critique to the way it approaches global public policies in the four areas of peace and security, promotion of civil and political rights, promotion of economic and social rights, and protection of the global environment. I start with benevolent imperialism.

Part II

Choosing Global Democracy

8

Benevolent Imperialism

BENEVOLENT IMPERIALISTS WANT THEIR country to use power to shape the world according to their own values. They believe that doing so is in the interest of both the world and their own country.

In the United States, benevolent imperialists include the so-called neoconservatives within the Republican Party. They want to use the unprecedented power of the U.S. government to promote democracy, human rights, peace, and free trade in the world, and to encourage allied nations to do the same. Neoconservatives represent a small faction of the foreign policy establishment, but it currently participates in power. They wielded a lot of influence in the first administration of George W. Bush, but have been largely discredited as a result of the quagmire in Iraq for which they are widely blamed.

Benevolent imperialism has some traction in the rest of the world as well. It has of course a long history in Europe and especially France and Britain. Although imperialism has now become a marginal idea in Europe, some politicians from across the political spectrum, such as former British Prime Minister Tony Blair or French Foreign Minister Bernard Kouchner, support the use of force to protect human rights (so-called humanitarian interventions), a position consistent with benevolent imperialism. At the other extreme, Islamist terrorism is also a form of benevolent imperialism, albeit one that seeks to promote an entirely different set of values. While Islamist terrorists' values are repellant to liberals, the point is that Islamists fight for what is, for them, an ideal. For the remainder of this book, though, I focus on the neoconservative version of benevolent imperialism.

Neoconservatives propose using international institutions to the extent that they can serve the United States' objectives. Otherwise they do not hesitate to ignore or undermine them. They are generally suspicious of the expansion of international institutions, and prefer to weaken them.

Neoconservatives do not regard global democracy, as I have defined it, desirable. Their conception of global democracy is the fostering of a community of democratic states. Implicit in this conception is that democracy should be limited to making national and local public policies. Global public policies should be shaped by the U.S. government, which should remain under the democratic control of U.S. nationals only, by virtue of its unparalleled military might.

THE ADAGE "POWER CORRUPTS and absolute power corrupts absolutely" represents a good general critique of benevolent imperialism. Benevolent imperialism cannot work, given human nature. The dream for enlightened kings has long proved a chimera. In the absence of adequate checks to excessive accumulation of power, benevolent imperialists fail to recognize mistakes they make, fail to see how their policies are driven by lowly interests rather than by the higher values they profess, and discount other people's values and interests.

The United States' response to the terrorist attacks of September 11, 2001, under the leadership of benevolent imperialists (as well as some nationalists), offers an illustration of that critique. I am going to delve into this issue in some detail in the next few pages, not only because it is the defining international affairs issue of our time, but also because it allows me to underscore a point that is too easy to underestimate: Lack of proper checks and balances in government is prone to generate very bad public policies—it can sometimes kill innocent civilians on a massive scale.

A few weeks after the attacks, President Bush said that he was amazed that so many foreigners hated Americans because "I know how good we are."[1] This statement set the tone for the so-called war on terrorism up to the time of publication of this book. The U.S. government has, to my knowledge, never publicly acknowledged that its past and present foreign policy could be part of the root causes of Islamist terrorism. That is regrettable. Although repression of terrorism is always warranted, it is also critical to address its root causes in order to undermine the legitimacy that terrorists might have among certain constituencies, thereby denting their recruitment and fundraising. Not even mainstream liberals spoke about the linkages between American foreign policy and the root causes of terrorism for months after September 11, 2001. Only the botched war against Iraq broke that silence, but it also allowed liberals to remain silent about other, past American foreign policies that fueled Islamist terrorism and that were endorsed by Democratic administrations.

In my own analysis—which was common among progressives on September 12, 2001, and is now more widely shared—Islamist terrorism is a dangerous ideology that has multiple causes but has unnecessarily gained momentum and become a global threat because of two root causes. It is in part a collection of traditional national liberation movements in countries where Muslims are or feel persecuted by repressive governments or foreign occupiers: Chechnya, Kashmir, Palestine, the Philippines, Afghanistan, Bosnia during the Yugoslav wars. In Iraq, violence can also be described in large part as the result of two Muslim groups (the Kurds and Shia Arabs) liberating themselves from a third one (the Sunni Arabs), who now themselves feel oppressed. There is even an element of "liberation movement" in European Islamist terrorism, as Muslim Europeans feel rejected from European societies. Although their struggles are local, these liberation movements build transnational networks among themselves both to exchange resources and as an expression of Muslim solidarity. To address this first root cause of Islamist terrorism, the international community needs to pressure the relevant governments to mitigate oppression of Muslims where it exists.

The second root cause of Islamist terrorism, intertwined with the first one but particularly relevant for countries where Muslims are not persecuted as a group, such as Saudi Arabia and Egypt, is a deep humiliation linked to the ascendance of the Western civilization over the Muslim one. For centuries Muslims wielded as much if not more power than Christians, but they became increasingly dominated culturally, economically, and militarily, starting with the European industrial revolution and culminating with European colonization of the Arab world and the United States' regional influence after the Second World War. In this view, the West is the enemy of Islamist terrorists, and Arab governments are seen as decadent and corrupt puppets of the West.

To address this second root cause of Islamist terrorism, the West must conduct a humble foreign policy toward the Muslim and particularly the Arab world. While it should not be apologetic for its economic ascendance and the appeal of its culture over traditional Arab culture, the West should be mindful of the many human rights violations it inflicted on Arab people in past decades, and should either avoid any new military interventions or ensure that they are seen as legitimate by Arab public opinion. Avoiding gross human rights violations is consistent with Western values anyway. While the West's cultural and economic ascendance may continue to generate a mix of resentment and envy, it is its foreign policy that really upsets Arabs.[2] When asked by a pollster: "What is your first thought when you hear 'America'?" an overwhelming majority of Arab respondents answered: "Unfair foreign policy."[3] And when asked: "What could the United States do to improve its image?" they answered: "Change its Middle East policy."

When planning the war against Iraq, the Bush administration and Blair government should have considered the history of abuse the West inflicted, directly or indirectly, on the Iraqi people. First, the British colonized them rather brutally.[4] Then the U.S. government and its European allies became accomplices of serious human rights violations committed by Saddam Hussein's regime.[5] They continued financing and selling arms to that regime even after it had executed thousands of opponents, attempted to invade a sovereign state (Iran), used weapons of mass destruction (chemical weapons) against enemy combatants as well as Iraqi civilians, and committed atrocities in Kurdistan that could amount to genocide.[6] President Bush completely ignored that history and the resentment it has left in Iraq and in the wider Muslim world, while at the same time condemning several Muslim governments for "supporting or harboring terrorists."[7] Such double standards go a long way in explaining rampant anti-Americanism in the Arab world, which, combined with the absence of legal ways to obtain redress, fuels Islamist terrorists' recruitment and fundraising efforts.

The problem is that there is little space, in the United States itself, for a debate on American human rights abuses in the rest of the world. Besides a fringe of people who read the progressive press, the American public is unaware of the responsibility of the U.S. government in serious human rights violations. Without any preexisting knowledge, there was no room on September 12, 2001, for any other discourse than one emphasizing patriotism, victimhood, righteousness, and incomprehension, which President Bush expressed when he said "I know how good we are."

Public debate about American responsibility in human rights violations is deficient in the United States because many foreign policies are bipartisan. There are nuances as well as some stark disagreements, most notably about the war against Iraq, when benevolent imperialists, nationalists, and multilateralists—whether Republicans or Democrats—have different appreciations of what constitutes the national interest. But, by and large, the national interest is indeed the interest of all Americans, whether Democrats or Republicans. Both parties then act as a block to pursue the national interest against the interest of foreigners, who do not get to vote for Congress and the presidency. When both parties speak with the same voice, the press has little room to report a variety of opinions. And when the foreign policy establishment is compromised in human rights violations, civil servants are also induced to remain silent in order to avoid jeopardizing their careers.

Given the bipartisan front on foreign policy within the United States, the main check on American policies should come from the rest of the world. But that check is quite weak considering the unparalleled power of the United States, particularly in the security policy area. For the most part, governments avoid public criticism of the U.S. government beyond some unwritten red lines, such as insinuating American complicity in serious human rights violations.

European governments are usually aligned with the U.S. government on the substance of foreign policy, even though they may have more nuanced positions or favor different tones and formalities. They usually criticize American foreign policy just enough to clear their own conscience, but not enough to change American behavior. The fuss over covert transport of terrorist suspects on European soil, which is a relatively minor human rights violation, is a good example. The opposition to the war against Iraq was an important exception in which some European governments put up a spirited opposition. But the French government had actually had an even closer relationship with Saddam Hussein than the U.S. government, which again limited its ability to fully spell out why Western troops would not be welcomed only with flowers by Iraqis.

Outside of Europe, governments are particularly vulnerable to American pressure and fear that public criticism would lead to American retaliation in such forms as forfeited trade agreements, cancelled World Bank loans, or meddling in their delicate domestic policy matters that could spark civil unrest. What the world really lacks are heads of government who, like Venezuela's President Hugo Chavez, are ready to pay the price of defying the United States but, unlike him, stick to fact-based and reasonable arguments and are excellent communicators by American standards. There is a lot of criticism about American foreign policy in the rest of the world, but as long as it is not relayed by governments in public and with some consistency, it fails to generate productive public debate inside the United States.

The combination of bipartisanship at home and reverence abroad creates a situation where the U.S. government can commit very serious human rights violations, such as the sanctions against Iraq between 1991 and 2003. Put in place by the administration of President George H. W. Bush, they were implemented by the United Nations (primarily during the Clinton administration), supported by the British, and either accepted or tolerated by all other governments. They were very harsh sanctions that killed hundreds of thousands of children and other vulnerable and innocent Iraqi people.[8] U.S. Secretary of State Madeleine Albright inadvertently told a journalist that the lives of half a million children were "a price to pay" to prevent Saddam Hussein from acquiring weapons of mass destruction.[9] This statement was a gaffe, as the U.S. government officially rejected any responsibility in the death of Iraqi children. But that gaffe points to the usually unspoken conventional wisdom that American policy makers are well sheltered from international humanitarian law, that they are accountable to American law and the American electorate only, and that it therefore makes sense for them to sacrifice hundreds of thousands of innocent foreigners in order to decrease the odds that an unknown number of American civilians might be killed in the future. While, during the same period, President Bill Clinton faced intense media scrutiny and a Congressional impeachment procedure for his lie about an extramarital sex affair, he had nothing to fear from the press, from the judicial system, or even less from Congress for his share of responsibility in the death of hundreds of thousands of Iraqi children.[10] The contrast between the Lewinsky affair and the sanctions against Iraq encapsulate in a nutshell the gap between the check-and-balance mechanisms that we take for granted at the national level of government and the dearth of them at the global level.

The case of abuses against prisoners at the Abu Ghraib facility in Iraq in April 2004 also contrasts with the earlier sanctions against Iraq. In the case of Abu Ghraib, the mainstream American press found the resolve to challenge the U.S. government on human rights grounds. The press rightly calculated that graphic television pictures showing clear-cut cases of human rights abuses would capture the passion of the American public. The fairly minor character of the human rights abuses (a few cases of humiliation and torture) also made it a fairly safe attack on foreign policy. (A wider pattern of torture and several cases of deaths in custody in Afghanistan, Iraq, and Guantanamo were reported later on.)[11] Human rights organizations had reported prisoner abuses in Afghanistan before the Abu Ghraib scandal,[12] as well as a large number of alleged deaths in custody of Taliban prisoners at the hands of allied Afghan militias.[13] But they did not receive the coverage they deserved by the mainstream press at the time. Only the television images of Abu Ghraib transformed prisoner abuse into a "story."

What the Abu Ghraib episode shows is that once the American public is properly educated, it has the right reaction of outrage. I do agree with President Bush when he says, "I know how good we are." The point of the above discussion on human rights violations committed or condoned by the U.S. government is not to accuse particular officials, but to condemn the lack of democracy at the global level of government. The tragedy is that power does corrupt even good people, and when it comes to global public policy making, the president of the United States wields tremendous power. The Bush and Clinton administrations' statements (quoted in notes 1, 7, and 9 in Part II) and the lack of uproar about them in the mainstream American press are astounding examples of the emperor being naked and nobody daring to shout it. From the perspective of Arab people, these statements must have seemed as outrageous as Mao Zedong's praise of the Great Leap Forward was to famished Chinese people.

Due to the dearth of check-and-balance mechanisms at the global level of government, it is hard for anyone to make a career in the State Department or in European chancelleries without becoming tainted with complicity in human rights violations. While nationalists or even multilateralists like President Clinton are subject to that critique as well, benevolent imperialists are the most exposed to it, because they want to undermine the weak check-and-balance mechanisms that do exist, and their whole approach to foreign policy making rests on the chimera of enlightened kings, which have never existed and never will.

By the time of writing, neoconservatives are widely discredited and blamed for their blindness and incompetence over the war in Iraq[14]—although not quite yet over their overall diplomacy toward the Muslim world. Americans have dared criticize their commander in chief only when the death toll of American troops has risen without credible prospects of prompt decline. But body count is a very imperfect check on presidential power. First, it is really only about American casualties: There is not much upheaval in the United States about the shocking Iraqi death toll (in the hundreds of thousands). Second, body count is a check mechanism that kicks in too late. Third, it is a mechanism that does not necessarily generate a productive course correction. While a case could be made for a measured withdrawal to prompt Iraqi leaders to take their own responsibilities, a hasty retreat from Iraq would not in itself generate a debate about the past history and overall relationship between the West and Islam, could give way to even more sectarian violence and Iraqi casualties, and could even embolden international terrorists.

THE GENERAL CRITIQUE OF benevolent imperialism—that good intentions go awry because power corrupts—applies to all areas of global public policy. In the areas of security and civil and political rights, benevolent imperialists want Western countries to wield their power to enforce peace and human rights worldwide, possibly through unilateral, preemptive attacks. In fact, benevolent imperialists have applied the doctrine of humanitarian intervention only to conflicts in which Western countries had an important interest. I have argued elsewhere that the war against Serbia over Kosovo in 1999, which was presented as a humanitarian intervention, was a case of good intentions corrupted by national interests.[15]

The only recent cases of genuine humanitarian interventions were the American intervention in Somalia in 1991 and the British intervention in Sierra Leone in 1999. But the former was the product of a somewhat frivolous decision by an outgoing president who had won a major war and opened a new geopolitical era full of hope. It foundered at the first American casualties, revealing a weak commitment to humanitarianism. And the latter succeeded with a very minor commitment of resources, which paradoxically also underscores a lack of commitment to pure humanitarianism because it shows that Western countries could wage very successful humanitarian wars in some circumstances, and yet fail to do so.

As to global economic policies, benevolent imperialists want the United States to use its power to promote free trade around the world, with the belief that it would benefit both the United States and other countries. However, the dearth of check-and-balance mechanisms in global trade policy making allow special interests to taint supposedly free trade policies. (It is arguable that genuinely free trade policies would help alleviate poverty anyway.) Benevolent imperialists are also favorable to foreign aid as an instrument of foreign policy. The Millennium Challenge Account created by the Bush administration is a mostly welcome addition to aid programs, although it is tainted by ideology as it fosters free-market economic policies that are not always good for poverty alleviation.

Finally, there is no clear benevolent imperialist orientation to global environmental policy, except for an aversion to such binding global regulations as the Kyoto Protocol of the Framework Convention on Climate Change.

9

Nationalism

NATIONALISTS, ALSO CALLED "REALISTS," consider that all states use their power in pursuit of their national interests. For them, balance-of-power politics is not only a descriptive, but also a prescriptive view of the world. They believe that it is the duty of national government officials to defend national interests, and that accepting international constraints on the exercise of power is not only undesirable, but also dangerous.

In the United States, nationalists represent a large faction of the foreign policy establishment, including many Republicans but also Democratic hawks. Nationalists have been present in every administration of the past decades, and they share power with benevolent imperialists in the Bush administration. I have mentioned that benevolent imperialism is tainted with nationalism, as the promotion of values often becomes corrupted by the pursuit of interests. Nationalism also taints the other approaches of foreign policy that I will examine, with nuances that I will explain in the next sections. Nationalism is a major foreign policy approach in every other country as well.

Like benevolent imperialists, American nationalists propose to use international institutions to the extent that they can serve the United States' objectives. Otherwise they do not hesitate to ignore or undermine them. They are generally suspicious of the expansion of international institutions, and prefer to weaken them. Again like benevolent imperialists, they do not regard democracy as desirable at the global level of government. But unlike them, they do not even aim at promoting national democracies worldwide unless it explicitly serves some national interests.

THE GENERAL CRITIQUE OF nationalism is that it is antithetical to most moral systems, including Judeo-Christian values. It is about celebrating egoism and deriding altruism as weakness. Although it may seem attractive to the people of the most powerful countries, the unmitigated pursuit of national interests has proved over the centuries to be a recipe for global mayhem. The history of international relations is nothing but a succession of wars brought about by exacerbated nationalism.

Nationalists retort that attempts at making foreign policy more ethical are dangerous and typically backfire because the rest of the world can exploit such overtures as weaknesses. They argue that the current overwhelming military superiority of the United States is a stabilizing, not destabilizing, factor in world politics. They have a point. Asia today, for example, looks much like Europe at the eve of the First World War, with nationalist tensions pitting militarily powerful states and territories against each other. There are the cold wars between North and South Korea, India and Pakistan, mainland China and Taiwan. There is also a strategic competition among China, India, Japan, Russia, and the United States for hegemony in the region. Multilateralists might like to believe that stronger international institutions as well as greater economic interdependence among all these states and territories prevent the emergence of an Asian version of the First World War. The nationalists' argument that American military might prevents such a devastating war seems much more plausible to me. In the next chapters I will argue that current international institutions' record at maintaining peace is abysmal.

While American power is part of the solution to maintaining peace, it is also part of the problem. An intrinsic aspect of nationalism is that the underdogs are always going to try toppling the top dog. American power understandably elicits both resentment and envy in the rest of the world. We are at a rare moment in history when, like Rome in ancient times, one power overwhelmingly dominates the world militarily, and somewhat less overwhelmingly dominates it economically and culturally. This situation may well continue for some decades. But it will not continue forever. Despite the stabilizing force of American military might in the foreseeable future, the spiral of American, Chinese, Japanese, and Russian nationalisms feeding each other is a very scary thing over a longer time horizon.[16]

Using American power to pursue American interests is dangerous in the long term, as it is certain to spur that spiral. By contrast, the benevolent imperialist project of using American power to promote a community of (national) democracies appears as more benign, as one might hope that relations among genuine democracies would be less problematic than relations among a mix of democracies and authoritarian regimes. But I have argued that benevolent imperialism is doomed because power corrupts. Besides, democracies can be very nationalistic as well—witness the United States or Japan.[17] A more effective way to break the dangerous spiral of nationalism is to promote democracy at the global level of government, not just at the national level.

NATIONALISM'S LACK OF ETHICAL compass is reflected in its prescriptions in all global public policy areas. In the area of peace and security, nationalists do not regard world peace as an objective. They are concerned only with security for their own nationals, and that may lead them to advocate preemptive wars and to foster conflicts among rival powers, such as the war between Iran and Iraq in the 1980s. Likewise, the promotion of civil and political rights worldwide is not an objective either, in sharp contrast with benevolent imperialism. The pursuit of national interests may well lead to the support of authoritarianism and to serious human rights violations abroad, such as the sanctions against Iraq already discussed.

In the area of global economic policies, alleviating poverty in the world is again not an objective for nationalists. It may sometimes be in the national interest to promote economic development in foreign countries, for example to strengthen an ally, just as it may be in the national interest to maintain potential rivals in poverty. For nationalists, foreign aid should be disbursed based on such foreign policy objectives, not based on needs. On global trade policy, nationalists adopt a mercantilist approach, favoring free trade in some industries and protectionism in others as it fits the interests of domestic companies. On global environmental policies, the goal is again to promote national interests, not the health of the whole planet. A powerful country that is also a big polluter, like the United States, should use its power to block global cooperation to reduce pollution.

ISOLATIONISM IS A VARIANT of nationalism. It shares its focus on national interests and suspicion of international institutions. But isolationists, such as Pat Buchanan, a U.S. presidential candidate in 1992, 1996, and 2000, have a different appreciation of what the national interest is. While nationalists usually advocate projecting power abroad, isolationists believe that aggressive foreign policies often entail more costs than benefits from a national interest perspective. Hence isolationists are weary of military interventions abroad and, compared to nationalists, have a stronger bias toward protectionism and against free trade.

10

Multilateralism

A THIRD CHOICE OF WORLD politics is multilateralism. Multilateralists, sometimes called "liberal internationalists," want states to solve global problems and resolve conflicts among their respective national interests within the framework of existing international institutions.

In the United States, multilateralists are dominant in the Democratic Party, but also include many Republican doves. Like nationalists, they represent a large faction of the foreign policy establishment and have been present in every administration of the past decades, although they are a minority in the Bush administration. Multilateralism is also an important foreign policy approach throughout the rest of the world, and the dominant one in Europe and some other countries.

For multilateralists, international institutions play a positive and important role in arbitrating competing national interests and in fostering global solutions to global problems. Multilateralists find existing international institutions roughly adequate, although they would generally welcome minor institutional reforms such as increased transparency and accountability of intergovernmental organizations, increased participation of civil society in those organizations, or the creation of new institutions as new global problems arise. They support the general concept of global democracy as long as it remains vague, or they actually claim that current institutions are democratic given the formal equality of states in most if not all international institutions, and given that representatives of states in intergovernmental organizations are accountable to elected national officials (at least in democracies).

THE GENERAL CRITIQUE OF multilateralism is twofold. First, while multilateralism purports to foster global solutions to global problems, the decision-making mechanisms of intergovernmental organizations are inadequate to meet global challenges. Most intergovernmental organizations existing at the global level are what I have defined as "weak confederations." Weak confederations allow states to free ride on global initiatives and do not enable intergovernmental organizations to impose the minimum discipline required to enforce global public policies (such as human rights conventions, for instance). The others are federations from the point of view of most states but strong confederations from the perspective of the United States and the Europeans, who can block any global initiatives. Given that solutions to most global problems require significant contributions from Western powers (in financial, military, or other terms), strong confederalism for the West can be as significant an impediment to global cooperation as weak confederalism for all.

Second, existing international institutions are also inadequate to fulfill the other goal of multilateralism: arbitrating conflicting national interests. Multilateralists do not reject the nationalists' claim that a state's foreign policy should pursue its national interests. After all, national officials are accountable to their national electorates, and pursuing national interests is therefore as natural for them as, say, maximizing profits is for managers of private enterprises. But multilateralists insist that the pursuit of national interests must take place within the framework of international institutions that level the playing field among states, again just as enterprises compete against each other within the boundaries of the law.

However, despite the apparent equality among states in most intergovernmental organizations thanks to the "one state, one vote" decision-making rule, there are actually huge imbalances of power among states within intergovernmental organizations. Inequality among states is what makes the multilateralists' claim on global democracy preposterous. Although, say, Bangladeshis may democratically control their representatives in intergovernmental organizations, the actual influence of these representatives at the World Trade Organization is marginal, and certainly not commensurate to their demographic weight, which happens to be equal to that of the Japanese. As a result, the World Trade Organization, which is supposed to level the playing field for the negotiation of international trade rules, often fails to do so, and sometimes even reinforces existing inequalities. Multilateralism is then analogous to insisting on the law to level the playing field among competing private enterprises, and then allowing Microsoft to write and enforce antitrust law.

Another example of the institutional failure to level the playing field, probably the most striking example of failure of the rule of law at the global level of government, is the one I used to discuss benevolent imperialism: the sanctions against Iraq between 1991 and 2003. They were approved by the United Nations, the multilateral body par excellence, but nevertheless violated international humanitarian law. President Clinton, who oversaw the sanctions over most of the period, was by and large a multilateralist, not a benevolent imperialist (although he did order the attack against Yugoslavia without United Nations authorization).

THAT TWOFOLD GENERAL CRITIQUE of multilateralism applies to all global public policy areas. Multilateralists want the international community to deliver peace and security throughout the world. But the United States and the Europeans use their veto power in the Security Council to escape their responsibilities in regions where they do not have important national interests (e.g., Africa), and to impose unbalanced solutions in regions where they have important interests (e.g., the former Yugoslavia in the 1990s).[18]

When NATO troops were poised to attack Serbia in 1999, journalist McGeary commented with wit on the factors influencing the international community's attitude toward rebellious ethnic minorities.[19] For instance, one of these factors is simply luck: "[Y]ou need to be in the right movement at the right time in the right place. The Kurds in Northern Iraq were just another bunch of bickering agitators until the

US needed them to challenge Saddam Hussein. [. . .] But Tamil Tigers of Sri Lanka: Your moment has yet to arrive." In reality, a very consistent behavior lies behind the Security Council's apparent double standards: The council will do what is in the interest of its permanent members, not what is needed to achieve world peace. Faced with this reality, McGeary concludes that, from the point of view of ethnic minorities, "war is still the best guarantee of independence—if you win. Eritrea won in 1993, after 32 years of battle. The Kosovars and the Kurds are not ready to concede."

The United Nations is very active in promoting peace in the world. Some intergovernmental organizations do play a useful role in preventing conflicts from escalating into violence, or in helping countries that emerge from violent conflicts not to fall back into them. But, in dealing with violent conflicts, the United Nations is allowed to play a meaningful role only when warring parties are exhausted, or only when one of them has managed to make a deal with the United States or another regional power such as France in Africa. Overall, the United Nations' record of peace enforcement over the past fifty years, or even in the post–Cold War era, has been dismal.

One could write a similarly scathing account of the biases of current international institutions in the other global public policy areas. Multilateralists want the international community to promote civil and political rights worldwide. But authoritarian governments escape their responsibilities by exercising their rights to opt out of human rights treaties. Since human rights institutions function according to the weak confederation model, the international community has basically no means to foster human rights in any meaningful way. Western powers rely on bilateral carrots and sticks to promote them, with evident biases (e.g., infinite patience with Saudi Arabia but a short temper with Iran).

Multilateralists want the international community to promote economic development worldwide, and in particular to eradicate extreme poverty. Poor nations have benefited from trade agreements and foreign aid in the past to some extent. However, the United States and the Europeans use their veto power to impose some rigged rules and double standards in global trade agreements that benefit them but harm poorer countries. They also exercise their rights to opt out of foreign aid commitments that are necessary to eradicate extreme poverty. Current aid commitments are not even sufficient to halve extreme poverty by 2015, which is nevertheless an official goal of the United Nations and its member-states. The quality of aid is also a victim of decision-making imbalances between rich donor nations and poor recipient ones.

Likewise, multilateralists want the international community to protect the global environment. But all states escape their responsibilities by exercising their rights to opt out of or weaken environmental treaties. As with human rights, global public policies to protect the environment are typically decided based on the weak confederation decision-making rule, which allows unfettered free riding.

All these failings of international institutions are structural. There is no reason to believe that multilateralism will fare better in the future than it has in the past. The gap between lofty declarations and reality is a built-in feature of multilateralism, which is a blend of ambitious and commendable global public policy objectives, with a dire lack of incentives for the members of the international community to work toward these objectives. In the end, all decisions are made by officials who are accountable to their own national electorates only. Nobody is accountable for the greater good of the planet and humankind.

11

Localism

A FOURTH CHOICE OF WORLD politics is localism. Localists want global public policies to leave space for local or national management of the economy, with an emphasis on sustainable development. Despite their preference for local or national public policies, however, localists are also strongly committed to the fulfillment of human rights throughout the world, including social, economic, and cultural rights. That is what distinguishes them from isolationists.

Localism is an approach to foreign policy that has a lot of support within the global movement for social justice (sometimes called the "anti-globalization movement"). I base my exposition of localism largely on the books *Alternatives to Economic Globalization*, *Localization*, and *A Possible World*.[20] Although the authors of the first book are prominent figures of that movement, they do not claim to represent it, and in fact a fundamental feature of the movement is that it tolerates and even nurtures a variety of opinions.

The global movement for social justice appeared in the 1990s. It has demonstrated its capacity to mobilize large numbers of people in rallies around the world, and has acquired considerable influence within a few years. However, it is not yet represented among the foreign policy establishments of major powers, although localists have started to make inroads in electoral politics in Latin America (e.g., Venezuela, Bolivia).

Localists have an ambivalent attitude toward international institutions. On the one hand, they have high aspirations for them, as they want these institutions to play an important role to fulfill human rights throughout the world. On the other hand, they resent the constraints that some international institutions place on local and national governments to manage the economy and environment. So they want international institutions to be supportive of, but not dictate, local and national public policy initiatives. In terms of the existing intergovernmental organizations, that means the following (in a nutshell):

- Shutting down or thoroughly transforming the International Monetary Fund, the World Bank, and the World Trade Organization
- Discarding veto rights at the Security Council and granting permanent member status to some large poor and middle-income countries;
- Maintaining the rest of the United Nations more or less as is, possibly with additional specialized agencies dedicated to global public policy areas such as antitrust laws (to restrain multinational companies) and controls on movement of capital (to transfer power from financial markets to national governments); such new institutions would presumably function along typical United Nations decision-making rules, such as lack of veto rights, extensive opt-out rights, and the "one state, one vote" distribution of voting rights.

Localists are strongly committed to democracy. They favor "bottom-up" or participatory decision-making processes that foster popular control of government at every level. They want to strengthen democracy at the local and national levels of government, thanks in part to the removal of global public policy constraints on local and national governments. They also strive to enact democracy at the global level by developing transnational civil society. The idea is that the burgeoning of contacts between nationals of various states should induce solidarity among them, such that national governments would transcend national interests for the common good of humankind.

WHETHER LOCALIZATION OF THE economy is an appropriate strategy to promote sustainable development is a debate that goes beyond the scope of this book. I personally believe that economic globalization can be a potent force for sustainable development, although many trade rules undermine that potential.[21] For the purpose of my present argument, however, my main critique of localism is that it lacks a comprehensive and coherent vision of global democracy. Books like *Alternatives to Economic Globalization* and *Localization* present alternative policy platforms that could by and large be carried out within existing institutions, if only more countries (especially powerful ones) were to follow the path of Venezuela and Bolivia and elect localist governments. In that sense, localism could almost be described as a variant of multilateralism—in the same way as I described isolationism as a variant of nationalism: It does not so much present a different conception of global government as a different platform for our existing global government.

The global movement for social justice has nevertheless advanced numerous proposals to reform international institutions. These proposals are well summarized in *A Possible World* and range from the creation of a People's Assembly at the United Nations to the strengthening of the World Social Forum itself (the main forum of the movement). However, they constitute a disparate list of proposals rather than a comprehensive and coherent vision. Moreover, *A Possible World* is actually a critical review that highlights many weaknesses in these proposals and the lack of a strong analytical framework to underpin them. In my opinion, most proposals suffer from either one or both of two flaws: Either the proposed institutions would be unlikely to lead to the intended outcomes in terms of improvements in global public policies, or they would not be as politically feasible as they might look at first sight.

The proposal to create an Economic Security Council, which is often included in blueprints to reform international institutions, illustrates both these flaws. The underlying idea is that the United Nations Security Council has enjoyed a higher profile and has been more effective (notwithstanding my critique in Chapter 10) than another United Nations organ: the Economic and Social Council (ECOSOC). Creating a new institution with a similarly high profile for the economic policy area is therefore deemed a good idea.

The role of the Economic Security Council would be the same as that of ECOSOC: providing overall leadership to all United Nations agencies on matters of global economic and social policies. Most authors advocating for it fail to explain why such a new body would be any more effective than ECOSOC itself. Neither the fancier name nor a smaller size would do much to increase effectiveness (the Security Council has only fifteen member-states, while ECOSOC has fifty-four members elected by the United Nations General Assembly). The key difference between ECOSOC and the Security Council is that the former is a weak confederation while the latter is a federation (albeit a strong confederation from the perspective of its permanent members, which is what makes it not so effective after all). Many authors proposing the creation of an Economic Security Council fail to specify whether it would be a federation like the Security Council. If it were not, it would be as ineffective as ECOSOC has been, as a majority of poor countries could press for deep reforms in global economic policies only to see rich countries opting out of them. If it were, as some authors have put forth, this proposal would be much more far-reaching than generally acknowledged.[22] Because it is based on familiar concepts (a mixture of ECOSOC and the Security Council), creating an Economic Security Council is generally presented as an incremental reform, while it would in fact be a change that would challenge the current balance of power as much as the vision of global democracy that I defend in this book, which I envisage developing over several decades. Moreover, a federal Economic Security Council would lack the check-and-balance mechanisms that are necessary in any democracy, which would make it much less likely to ever be instituted than the global democratic reforms I propose in Chapter 12. It is hard to imagine the member-states of the United Nations delegating all powers on global economic policies to a small subset of member-states. Citizens and special interests of the few elected countries would be in a much better position to manipulate the system to their own advantage than citizens and industries of the rest of the world.

The lack of coherent alternatives for international institutions renders the localist project precariously dependent upon the enlightened leadership of localist leaders at the national level of government, and upon the pressures of the global movement for social justice itself. Venezuela's President Chavez has demonstrated that he was able to transcend the interests of his electorate and share Venezuela's oil wealth through economic agreements with countries ruled by sympathetic governments (i.e., Cuba, Bolivia), forming the Bolivarian Alternative for the Americas. It is nevertheless a big act of faith to believe that such altruistic arrangements could form a sustainable and universal basis for international relations. At the end of the day, even localist leaders would come under strong pressures to defend national interests at the expense of their neighbors' interests (especially those leaders who cannot rely on oil reserves).

Global civil society can pressure national governments to foster such enlightened leadership transcending national interests, but again it is daring to assume that the global movement for social justice would have sufficient influence on most countries (especially the most powerful ones) most of the time. In the absence of enlightened leadership, powerful countries would be able to exploit weak confederalism and escape their responsibilities to deal with global challenges.

THIS GENERAL CRITIQUE OF localism plays itself out in each global public policy area. Like multilateralists, localists want the international community to deliver peace with security throughout the world. But discarding veto rights and changing the membership of the Security Council would probably not productively change the biases of that body, which I highlighted when discussing multilateralism. For even if a majority of poor and middle-income countries could force certain decisions onto the United States and its European allies, the latter would retain control over the lion's share of the means to implement these decisions: military might. The Security Council's decisions could simply go unenforced, which would undermine its authority.

More generally, even a reformed Security Council would lack adequate check-and-balance mechanisms to be entrusted with the most vital of all decisions: declaring war. The nonpermanent members would also have vested interests that might be detrimental to the just resolution of particular armed conflicts. Some members could be directly affected positively or negatively by a given conflict. When Syria was elected to the council from 2002 to 2004, it was judge and party on the Middle East conflict, for instance. Others might seek to sell their votes in exchange for concessions on some unrelated issues. For example, both France and the United States tried to buy votes from nonpermanent members for the failed resolution to authorize the war against Iraq in 2003.[23] The bottom line is that would-be localist governments may well drive the Security Council toward more ethical global security policies, but they would also be subject to the corruption of power in the face of weak check-and-balance mechanisms. The support of the German Green Party, which can be described as close to the global movement for social justice, for the war against Yugoslavia in 1999 is a worrying sign in that respect.

Again like multilateralists, localists want the international community to promote human rights worldwide. Although their commitment to human rights is very strong, the role they would like to see international institutions playing in fulfilling them is unclear. In general, localists espouse the weak confederation decision-making rule, such that intergovernmental organizations would probably not have any more leverage on national governments than they do today.

In the economic area, localists favor economic and social policies developed at the national or lower levels of government, using resources mainly from those national or lower levels. However, to the extent that states would not become totally self-sufficient, they would continue to rely on international cooperation to fulfill the economic and social rights of their peoples. The United States and the Europeans would continue to have the upper hand in international negotiations thanks to their economic wealth and military power, whether or not such negotiations take place in the intergovernmental organizations that localists want to close down, such as the World Trade Organization or the International Monetary Fund. In the end, formal inequalities within existing intergovernmental organizations merely reflect real power imbalances; they do not cause them. Experience shows that rich countries can extract even more concessions from poor ones in bilateral and regional free-trade agreements than at the World Trade Organization. That said, localists could argue that unfair trade rules would not hurt the national economy much in a situation of near-autarky.

It is worth noting that every state already has the right not to join or to secede from the International Monetary Fund, the World Bank, and the World Trade Organization. Every state can also default on its debts and adopt far-reaching regulations of international trade and investment to be enforced on its territory. The consequences of such policy choices would be sharp decreases in trade flows and inward foreign investments—but neither of these consequences would be negative from a localist perspective. (A more negative consequence would be an outflow of domestic capital, which could devastate those national economies that face high financial risks to start with. National governments can impose restrictions on capital outflows, but, unless governments of countries in which capital flows in cooperate, these controls can be evaded. An international agreement committing most if not all states to cooperate in controlling capital flows is therefore the key missing international institution that would help national governments espouse the localist development model.)

In the area of global environmental policies, localism faces the same problem as it does for human rights policies: Its strong commitment to protecting the environment is not matched by proposals for better international institutions to enforce global rules. National or local management of the economy with an emphasis on sustainability should reduce the acuteness of global environmental problems. But some environmental problems such as climate change or loss of biodiversity do require disciplined action at the global level of government.

In sum, localists lack a comprehensive and coherent vision for global democracy. In particular, they face a real tension between ambitious global objectives on the one hand, and a preference for national or local decision making on the other hand.

12

Global Democracy

THE FIFTH AND NEW choice that I propose for world politics is global democracy. I define global democracy as the application of key concepts of liberal representative democracy to the global level of government, which would happen incrementally over several decades by developing institutional innovations already adopted by some international institutions.

This approach to foreign policy is only emerging, and it is not yet an organized political force in any country. Europeans are likely to be more receptive to this approach because they have espoused it at their regional level. The development of the European Union is very much in line with global democracy. Ever since the end of the Second World War, European integration has actually been the most important source of innovative institutional arrangements that could inspire global democracy, though by no means the only one. However, Europeans have shown few signs of promoting global democracy in their relations with the rest of the world. They remain mostly multilateralists in that regard.

Global democracy is supportive of strong international institutions, but calls for radical—though incremental—reforms of existing institutions. In summary, I believe that intergovernmental organizations should progressively move toward the adoption of the following nine institutional features (using terminologies explained in Part I):[24]

1. Two-tiered institutional architecture

New, second-tier intergovernmental organizations should allow pioneer-ing states to take on deeper commitments of international cooperation, while less committed states could remain members of existing, first-tier organizations. This feature is necessary because we start from a situation of great distrust and even enmity among some states. Universal organiza-tions like the United Nations are therefore unlikely to nurture the close, trustful collaboration that global democracy implies. Rather, global de-mocracy can be developed through incremental institutional reforms in a variety of existing and new intergovernmental organizations, based on shared interests and values among subsets of states.

2. Secession rights

States should keep the right to leave or not to join any intergovernmental organizations (whether first- or second-tier ones). Secession rights are the ultimate check on excessive power by intergovernmental organizations.

3. Limited opt-out rights

Opt-out rights (i.e., the right for states not to implement decisions of intergovernmental organizations while remaining a member of them) should generally be limited in second-tier intergovernmental organiza-tions because they hinder the effectiveness of global public policies. Some opt-out rights could nevertheless be preserved to allow for flexible in-cremental reforms. In particular, I will explore the notion of authorized opt-out rights, or the right of member-states not to implement particular decisions of intergovernmental organizations with the explicit assent of the other member-states.

4. Limited veto rights

Veto rights (i.e., the right for any single member-state to block decisions) should be avoided in second-tier intergovernmental organizations, except perhaps for "constitutional amendments," that is, changes in the statutes of the intergovernmental organizations. Veto rights should especially be avoided in organizations that have large memberships because they tend to generate paralysis, and they should not be attributed to some member-states but not others because that is not fair. Together with the limits on opt-out rights, limiting veto rights means that second-tier intergovernmental organizations would be mostly federal organizations.

5. Human rights entry tests

States desiring to join second-tier intergovernmental organizations should comply with minimum standards of civil and political rights as defined by these organizations. This feature is necessary because global democracy cannot exist without democracy at the national level: If national governments are not democratic, they cannot represent their nationals in intergovernmental organizations with full legitimacy; if citizens cannot participate in national politics, they are unlikely to be able to participate in global politics.

6. Free entry

Membership of second-tier intergovernmental organizations should be open to all applying states, provided that they agree to abide by their rules, including human rights entry tests and limited opt-out rights. This feature is necessary to ensure the propagation of global democracy throughout the world. Rejecting states that are ready to abide by the rules of an intergovernmental organization is tantamount to declaring them as second-class entities, which fuels resentment.

7. Equal universal suffrage (one person, one vote) and majority voting

Decisions of second-tier intergovernmental organizations should be taken by the majority of the member-states' combined populations, possibly with various degrees of qualifications (e.g., supermajority requirements for sensitive decisions). Majority voting and equal universal suffrage remain at the core of democracy and should therefore be at the core of global democracy. But supermajorities are warranted for "constitutional amendments," such as transfers of competences that change the boundaries between the national and global public interests.

8. Independent judiciary

Second-tier intergovernmental organizations should have independent judicial organs, whose decisions should override those of national courts. Although mediation, arbitration, and other peaceful conflict resolution mechanisms have their merits, adjudication by independent and professional judges on the basis of codified law or legal precedent has proved immensely helpful to democracy at the national level of government. In particular, mediation and other conflict resolution techniques used by most existing international institutions fail to redress imbalances of power between parties, which compromises the fairness of settlements. Adjudication can of course only work when court decisions can be enforced. In accordance with the first feature of global democracy (i.e., two-tiered institutions), the enforcement mechanism to uphold judiciary decisions of second-tier intergovernmental organizations should be to expel noncomplying member-states, in which case the underlying conflict would be dealt with under the rules of existing, first-tier international institutions, even if that results in less effective or less fair settlements.

9. Generalism

Separate functional intergovernmental organizations should progressively consolidate to form general organizations, that is, organizations dealing with several global public policy areas at the same time, such as security, human rights, environment protection, and economic development. This feature is important because it allows for cross-issue bargaining under the same democratic rules. Representatives of different states can make compromises across a large variety of issues on the basis of a fair distribution of power. By contrast, functionalism allows for undemocratic "off-the-table" bargaining, as states are able to take advantage of their unfair voting power in one organization (e.g., the World Bank) to buy votes in another (e.g., the International Atomic Energy Agency).

Each of these nine institutional features already exists in some intergovernmental organizations, as shown throughout Part I. Only the European Union includes all of them, except that the fifth feature (free entry) is limited to states located on the European continent—an important qualification! I will show in Part III how various existing intergovernmental organizations might develop some of these features in the coming decades, at various speeds and with various sequencing, or how new organizations with such features might be created, in order to improve the way in which the international community deals with securing peace; promoting civil, political, economic, and social rights; and protecting the global environment.

Before moving to this more detailed discussion, however, I think it is worth presenting a broad critique of global democracy at this point. The most important critique is that the move to more federalism would obviously reduce the diversity of public policies, which would be regrettable because preferences over public policies vary across states. Even if global public policies were decided by the majority of the combined populations of the members-states of a given intergovernmental organization, they may not be liked by the majorities of the populations of some of those member-states. For example, some nations are ready to pay a higher price to avert climate change than others, and the former would prevail under the majority rule if they were more populous. Although I will show in Part III that federalism would not necessarily lead to one-size-fits-all policies, one of the goals of global democracy is to induce states to make compromises among their conflicting preferences. The enthusiasm for coal-powered plants of one country must somehow be tempered by the fear of rising sea levels of another.

Moreover, many global public policies deal with issues that are not obviously global issues, such as regulations of foreign investment in the health sector (which in many countries is tightly managed by the national government). It would be even harder for minorities to accept the global majority rule on issues that they deemed fundamentally national in character. Since there are no objective criteria to assign issues at national or supranational levels, competences of various levels of government should be continuously negotiated among and within states. Existing federal intergovernmental organizations such as the European Union and the World Trade Organization are constantly undergoing such acrimonious negotiations. Nevertheless, that critique should be put in perspective. Democracy, because it relies on the rule of the majority, necessarily produces frustrated minorities. But, in the end, that is better than a frustrated majority.

What would be vital to global democracy is that citizens remain loyal to its overall institutional framework, including the limits it would put on majority rule. This framework would consist of both their own state's constitution and the treaties to which it adhered. The right to secession would be an important, ultimate guarantee to ensure that loyalty be preserved. Supermajorities (if not veto rights) to add or subtract competences of intergovernmental organizations would also be important limits to the majority rule. In that respect, it is worth noting that global democracy would not be incompatible with localism. The majority of the world's population could prefer localist policies. And if that were not the case, nations that would prefer localist policies would be able to choose to remain outside of most second-tier intergovernmental organizations, except perhaps those dealing with issues such as antitrust laws or controls on capital movements. They could contribute to the solution of global problems through continued international collaboration within the framework of first-tier institutions.

From the importance of the secession right flows a second limitation of global democracy. Its development would depend on the continuous support of a critical mass of nations, preferably including powerful ones. It would be easy for powerful national governments to bypass global democratic institutions and continue making global public policy in other forums. In that sense, global democracy is a general attitude or approach to foreign policy making, not just a set of institutional reform proposals. It consists of a set of decision-making rules as well as a willingness to play by those rules.

I criticized localism on the ground that its success hinged on the permanent presence of enlightened leaders in most national governments, including the most powerful ones. That criticism therefore applies to global democracy as well. However, it is much less potent in the case of global democracy. Once some global democratic institutions were established and became a normal part of world politics, shaping the expectations of all global actors, it would become much harder for global elites to break global democratic rules than to change a particular global public policy (e.g., dismantling import tariffs). In other words, it is harder to act egoistically when that implies rejecting a set of rules widely regarded as fair than it is to act egoistically in the absence of rules.

Like nationalism and multilateralism, global democracy would allow national governments to pursue national interests. But unlike nationalism, global democracy would demand that such pursuit be bound by rules; and unlike multilateralism, it would demand that these rules be decided democratically. Global democracy would require some selflessness on the part of rich and powerful countries to accept democratic rules in the first place, but then would allow them to be selfish within the boundaries of these rules. Localism, on the other hand, requires complete and constant selflessness, which cannot realistically be expected.

A third general critique of global democracy, emanating from the right of the political spectrum, is that it would imply a huge transfer of power from rich countries to heavily populated and poor ones. That is the point. It would be a good thing from an ethical point of view. Equality of political rights lies at the core of democracy, and if poor people happen to be the ones who currently enjoy inferior political rights (unsurprisingly, as history teaches us), they should be empowered. Critics may say that global democracy would merely transfer power from two superpowers—the United States and the European Union—to two others—China and India. That would still make three times more empowered people. Besides, I will show that global democracy does not necessarily mean transferring power to the national governments of populous countries: Power might instead be transferred to transnational groups representing the interests of many people (a high proportion of whom would be either Chinese or Indian).

That said, significant income and wealth inequalities may create dangerous instabilities in the democratization process of intergovernmental organizations, and therefore they do call for incrementalism, which is salient in the notion of global democracy that I advocate. The secession right to which I have already referred would guarantee that any transfer of power would not be reckless, but rather the product of sustained moral pressure and well-understood self-interest.

The fourth general critique of global democracy, also emanating from the right of the political spectrum and particularly from benevolent imperialists and nationalists, is that it would be too dangerous. In his book *Of Paradise and Power*, Robert Kagan argues that multilateralism is a nice idea in theory but one that can thrive in Europe only because Americans do not hesitate to ignore international institutions when push comes to shove in relations with antagonistic and illiberal governments.[25] But global democracy would not be multilateralism. I will show in Part III that global democracy would allow for decisive action to maintain security, without curtailing options to deal with threats such as international terrorism and the proliferation of weapons of mass destruction. Global democrats need not be doves.

Finally, the fifth general critique of global democracy emanates from the left of the political spectrum. It argues that liberal representative democracy is not perfect, and that a global democracy inspired by it could therefore not be perfect either. In particular, the existence of global civil and political rights would not necessarily imply that disadvantaged members of global society would be able to exercise them effectively to pursue their interests. I am intimately aware that that is correct. The choice of global democracy that I propose is only part of the solution to empower marginalized people. A vibrant and inclusive civil society would be necessary both to make global democracy happen in the first place, and to ensure that it would work. Even though it may not end up working better than democracy at the national level of government does, global democracy would nevertheless represent a major improvement compared to the current global apartheid.

ALTHOUGH GLOBAL DEMOCRACY IS not a panacea, it is a coherent alternative approach to foreign policy, which, as I am now going to argue, could improve the way the international community would deal with the global challenges of promoting peace, human rights, and sustainable economic development.

Part III

Applying Global Democracy

13

Promotion of Peace and Security

NOW THAT I HAVE explained in detail what I mean by global democracy and have argued that political equality at the global level is a human right, I am going to explore various scenarios showing how existing international institutions could incrementally evolve toward global democracy over the coming decades. Considering current preferences, interests, conflicts, and disagreements among national and transnational groups, I will argue that global democracy would produce global public policies that, overall, would be better to deal with today's global challenges of achieving world peace, promoting human rights and economic development, and protecting the global environment. I am also going to discuss the political forces that could bring about the institutional changes I advocate. I start with the policy area of peace and security, which remains the primary driver of international relations.

What is the global democratic approach to peace and security?

The first feature of global democracy is a two-tiered institutional architecture, allowing cohesive groups of states to pioneer deeper international cooperation to help solve global problems. As far as global security policies are concerned, the first tier of institutions would consist of the existing United Nations Security Council, other relevant United Nations organs, as well as regional intergovernmental organizations like the African

Union. The United Nations would continue functioning as it currently does, and I have argued that we should not expect major improvement in its effectiveness because it suffers from deep structural, institutional deficiencies.

That is why I propose to expand either the North Atlantic Treaty Organization (NATO) or the European Union (or both) to serve as second-tier intergovernmental organizations to promote global security. Other regional intergovernmental organizations, or new ones created by any combination of states, could (re)orient themselves to play that role as well, following a path similar to the one I am going to sketch for NATO and the European Union. However, NATO and the European Union are by far the most credible organizations to fulfill that role at this time.

Ever since the end of the Cold War, NATO has been searching for a new mission and has been tempted to play the role of "global cop." The global democratic way to play that role would be to transform NATO from an exclusive club of rich and militarily powerful countries into an organization open to all states (feature 6: free entry). There exists a precedent of enlargement, as NATO welcomed a number of states from Central and Eastern Europe in the 1990s. But to become a legitimate global police, NATO would need to enlarge its membership beyond the North Atlantic region, obviously requiring a change of name.

I envisage three waves of enlargement. The first wave could happen fairly soon and would include countries that are already close allies of existing NATO members-states, such as Australia and New Zealand, Japan and South Korea (with the caveat that relations with North Korea must be carefully managed), and Mexico. Most of these countries (and others) already have formal partnership agreements with NATO and collaborate on the ground in several operations. The second wave would require more confidence-building time and would include relatively stable democratic states, including many states of Latin America and some states of Africa and Asia (e.g., India, Senegal, South Africa, Thailand). The third wave would start even later and include states that are not currently stable democracies, but that could become such in the coming decades. As specified by feature 6 (free entry), NATO would not select its new members-states, but all states willing to join would be admitted provided that they accepted all NATO policies.

The primary policy of NATO is to consider any attack on one member-state as an attack on all member-states, and therefore to commit all necessary resources to defend any member-state. Other NATO defense policies could themselves be strengthened in several ways:

- *Minimum defense spending*: There is an expectation among NATO member-states to maintain sufficient armed forces to contribute to the security of all members. But that expectation is currently not quantified, and members (especially smaller ones) tend to free ride on the defense investments of others. A larger NATO, spanning several continents, would make that collective action problem more acute. Enlargement would be an opportunity to revisit and strengthen rules of burden sharing for both existing and new members.
- *Greater specialization of national forces*: NATO directly manages a number of military assets, and member-states are also expected to coordinate investments in other assets, to minimize duplication. Unlike minimum defense spending requirements, specialization is hard to codify, but it should nevertheless continue to be promoted as NATO enlarges. That would increase the defense interdependence of NATO member-states. National armies, especially those of small states, would progressively cease to be self-sufficient, which would foster solidarity among member-states.
- *Border disputes*: Referring any border dispute to the International Court of Justice could become a condition of NATO membership. This is not currently the case, and the navies of two NATO members, Greece and Turkey, have been posturing over their disputed sea border. The potential for such tensions would increase as NATO enlarged, and could seriously undermine the alliance. Resolving border disputes is the one thing for which the International Court of Justice has been effective over the past sixty years.
- *"New threats"*: NATO membership could also become conditional to the ratification of a number of United Nations treaties relevant to peace and security, including those on arms control (e.g., the Nuclear Proliferation Treaty), terrorism, and international crime.

NATO could itself develop tighter treaties, to be adopted by its own membership and to be expanded to the rest of the world through negotiations under the auspices of the United Nations. Authorized opt-out rights would allow for some flexibility in the adoption of such treaties (e.g., the United States keeping the right to lay mines in the Demilitarized Zone in Korea despite the treaty banning land mines).

There are four ideas behind this set of tighter NATO policies. First, tighter rules would be necessary to preserve discipline and cohesion as the number of member-states increased, and especially as NATO started to welcome states that existing members might not trust as fully as they currently trust each other.

Second, these rules would encourage potential members to abide by global security policies, such as United Nations treaties on arms transfers. The experience of the European Union shows that the prospect of membership to a coveted club is a powerful incentive for would-be members to adopt international rules. These first two points are aligned with feature 3 of global democracy: limiting opt-out rights to ensure enforcement of global policies.

Third, these rules would make it easier to expel some states from NATO. Termination of membership is not imaginable under NATO's current model as a select club but it should become a possibility in grave circumstances as the number of NATO states increases to a large number, again to preserve discipline and mutual accountability among member-states and protect NATO's defense credibility. If attempts at mediation or arbitration of conflicts among member-states fail, an independent judiciary (feature 8 of global democracy) should be able to ascertain important breaches of NATO policies by some of its member-states and recommend termination of their memberships.

The fourth idea is that NATO would become a forum for its members to debate and agree on a common approach to global security policy, which they would then negotiate with nonmembers in the various first-tier forums such as the United Nations Security Council. NATO already serves as a forum for dialogue and consensus-building for its member-states. But NATO member-states do not necessarily speak with one voice in other intergovernmental organizations, and that would become increasingly necessary, as I will explain below.

In addition to adopting NATO's security policies, existing and new member-states alike should also meet minimum standards of civil and political rights. The promotion of freedom and human rights has always been a core objective of NATO. Yet several of its member-states have been dictatorships at some point (i.e., Greece, Portugal, Spain, and Turkey). By contrast, the European Union has played an important role in encouraging these same dictatorships to democratize. It did so by specifying a clear list of civil and political liberties that all potential members had to meet in order to be admitted, and by setting up a court to enforce that entry test (features 5 and 8). Any citizen of a state that is member of the European Union can sue his or her own government in a European court after having exhausted national appeals.

By adopting such a strong human rights entry test, NATO would confirm its identity vis-à-vis the rest of the world: an organization aiming not just at maintaining peace but also at promoting a certain vision of a just society, one where civil and political liberties prevail. Combined with free entry (feature 6), the human rights entry test (feature 5) would basically mean that all states protecting the civil and political liberties of their citizens would be worth defending, and hence automatically admitted.

Free entry with the human rights entry test would also reassure states that may not contemplate early membership, thereby decreasing tensions between NATO and the rest of the world. Currently, NATO defines its friends, that is, its potential members, somewhat arbitrarily. By the same token, it defines its potential enemies, that is, states that are ruled out as members, somewhat arbitrarily as well. That can vex the potential enemies and induce them to become actual enemies.

For example, NATO and the Serbian government have dramatically improved their relations since their war of 1999. But that was not a foregone development and is still reversible. A hard-line nationalist party could win elections in Serbia. At the same time, Croats could elect a government that could be more liberal in its economic policies though not necessarily in its protection of civil and political rights. If that were to be the case, and if one also took into account historical prejudices on both sides, there would be a good chance that NATO would treat Serbia less kindly than Croatia. Serbia would then treat NATO less kindly in return, generating a spiral of conflict that could again destabilize the region.

By contrast, a global democratic approach would have NATO diffuse some of the tension by offering, as a matter of policy, automatic membership to both Serbia and Croatia provided that they respected a specific list of civil and political liberties and referred border disputes to the International Court of Justice. In sum, the human rights entry test enforced by independent courts adds objectivity to what can otherwise be a subjective or even politically motivated assessment of a state's commitment to peace and human rights.

The human rights entry test would also be necessary to deal with civil unrest or civil wars within NATO members. Were NATO to expand, the risk of civil wars inside one of its member-states would increase, which could seriously destabilize the defense alliance. Turkey has known a civil war in its Kurdish provinces, which has put the other NATO members in a situation where they were condoning serious human rights violations.

Besides expanding geographically and tightening its defense policies and human rights entry test, a third area of reform that NATO would need to undergo in order to play a prominent role in global security policy in a global democratic way concerns its decision-making processes. NATO does not legislate. But it does make a wide variety of important decisions that affect people's security, such as adopting general defense doctrines or plans for the geographic deployment of national armed forces. Its current decision-making rules range from strong to weak confederalism. NATO's top organ, the Council, takes decisions by consensus, in other words, all member-states have a veto right. But while member-states face a strong expectation, if not a legal constraint, to implement some decisions, other decisions represent guidelines that member-states may or may not implement. In other words, member-states enjoy opt-out rights for some decisions but not others. The best example between this combination of strong and weak confederalism pertains to the decision of committing NATO to a particular crisis outside the North Atlantic zone (e.g., Bosnia). All members must agree for a mission to be created, but members have a large degree of latitude to commit their own troops.

There is no pressing need to review these decision-making rules at this time. But I have argued that, were NATO to expand, there would be a strong case for limiting opt-out rights to preserve the cohesion of the alliance (feature 3). The sheer number and diversity of members would also make a strong case for limiting veto rights (feature 4), because paralysis might otherwise set in, and paralysis would be very dangerous for a defense alliance. In other words, expanding NATO while maintaining its effectiveness would require a progressive move toward federal decision making. Consistent with the concept of global democracy presented in Chapter 12, federal decision making should take place in the form of majority rule with votes weighted by population (feature 7).

As was the case with the European Union, majority rule could be established gradually, by limiting it to fairly minor decisions and by relying on qualified majority votes (e.g., a two-thirds majority) to start with. Even when the simple majority and equal universal suffrage were established formally, real power would be transferred only gradually. The U.S. government would continue to call the shots for a long time for several reasons. First, the United States is a big country, with a third of the total population of the current NATO area. Under current membership, an alliance with "new Europe" (i.e., Central European countries and Britain) would give it a simple majority if votes were exactly proportional to population, for instance. As new members are brought in, the United States would of course need to secure more allies. And if a demographic giant like India were to become a NATO member at a time when the United States had not yet fully embraced the majority rule at the global level of government, a transitional voting system would be called for. For example, both India and the United States could have a veto right, such that all NATO decisions would require approval of the United States, India, and a simple majority of all other member-states by equal universal suffrage (one person, one vote).

Second, the United States' influence would surpass its share of votes. Its "soft" power derived from its strong economy and cultural influence would remain assets allowing the United States to forge winning alliances with ease, whether with existing or new member-states.

Third and foremost, given that America's military might would be the primary asset of NATO, the shadow of American secession from NATO, even if not explicitly threatened, would also dissuade other member-states from confronting American intransigence on important issues, at least as long as the principle of majority voting became strongly established through a practice of voting on minor decisions.

Ultimately, the most sensitive decision that NATO would need to take through majority rule would be the authorization of offensive use of force or the imposition of sanctions against non-member-states. In defensive situations (e.g., war against Afghanistan in retaliation for its support of the terrorist attacks of September 11, 2001), there should be no controversy: All member-states would defend the member-states that were attacked as a matter of policy and treaty obligation, and those that failed to do so would be expelled from the organization. In offensive situations, by contrast, the North Atlantic Treaty currently states that the alliance's foreign policy, and that of its member-states, must be compatible with United Nations policies. In practice, that leaves room for serious disagreements, as the war against Iraq in 2003 demonstrated.

Two camps with fundamentally different appreciations of the threat posed by Iraq emerged within NATO. One camp, led by the United States, pressed forward with the argument that failure to disarm Iraq by force would endanger all; the other, led by France, countered that a premature allied attack against Iraq would feed the resolve of Islamist extremism and hence endanger all. In other words, both camps argued that reckless action by the other camp would be a threat to all. It is very important for a defense alliance that member-states pursue compatible foreign policies vis-à-vis nonmembers. NATO was very effective during the Cold War thanks to a strong convergence of views among its member-states about the Soviet threat. But foreign policy disagreements like the Iraq case could potentially lead NATO to its death. The war against Iraq may or may not have marked the beginning of a long-term transatlantic rift. In any case, the expansion of the alliance to new members, combined with the greater diversity of threats compared to the Cold War era, would certainly increase the potential for major foreign policy disagreements among NATO members. The way the Iraq case was resolved was that some NATO members acted unilaterally, outside of the purview of NATO (and without explicit Security Council authorization). That has undermined solidarity among NATO member-states as some states are feeling indirectly threatened by their allies' recklessness.

The global democratic way to address that important problem would be to transform NATO from a purely defense-oriented alliance to an organization that would both commit to defend its members and authorize (or not) offensive actions by its members against nonmembers. NATO member-states would not be allowed to act offensively outside of the framework of NATO (feature 3: no opt-out rights). And they would jointly decide to authorize the use of force or to impose sanctions against nonmembers by majority vote with votes weighted by population (feature 7). Dissenting members would have to accept the decision of the majority and assume collective responsibility for it—or leave the organization. NATO would then become the primary forum for foreign policy formulation for all its member-states. While the other proposals I have advanced so far could be implemented incrementally, this one looks like a revolution at this time, and it would remain a major step even as the culmination of the long process of institutional reforms outlined above. As President Bush made clear—"America will never seek a permission slip to defend the security of our country"—it would be politically very difficult, to say the least, for the U.S. government to accept it.

Yet I am optimistic that such power sharing between the U.S. government and its allies could happen during my lifetime (I am young). U.S. foreign policy does affect the security of people throughout the world, for the better but also for the worse, and allies of the United States are unlikely to continue accepting it as a fact of life. President Bush's confident "permission slip" sound bite already rings hollower today concerning Iran than it did just three years ago about Iraq—although it will take decades before a U.S. president dares acknowledging that she does actually need such a slip.

In *America's Inadvertent Empire*, William Odom and Robert Dujarric recommend that American decision makers "consider America's allies [. . .] as full stake-holders of the empire. That means allowing them to influence U.S. policy making and strategy, though not always to make policy and strategy."[1] To me, as a European citizen, that statement reads like a polite invitation to accept second-class citizenship. And it echoes a terser line by Ignacio Ramonet, president of the French foreign affairs magazine *Le Monde Diplomatique*: "An empire does not have allies; it only has vassals." Nationals of small European states like my own, Belgium, have accepted being America's vassals during the Cold War era, although they are now waking up to it. The British, whose former leader embodies vassalage more than any other person, are ambivalent about that status. The French have always had a very hard time bearing it, and many are in a state of denial about it, which regularly vexes Americans. And if vassalage was all that was on offer to reward friendlier behavior by proud Chinese or Iranians, I understand that they would prefer remaining respectively "strategic competitor" and "state of concern," that is, potential and actual enemies. Russia has been weakened since the end of the Cold War, and India has not quite yet risen to its potential, but both are likely in the decades to come to expect a status in world politics other than U.S. vassal. Even Japan, which has accepted vassalage for half a century due to a humiliating military defeat, is unlikely to remain there. Promoting democracy at the national level, which is a core objective of benevolent imperialists, would not decrease the resentment of the Chinese or Russians about being treated as second-class global citizens. Indeed, Russia's loss of global influence has arguably undermined the democratization of its national government. Global democracy is the best way to induce big powers to consider a course other than confrontation with the United States.

I must emphasize that what would be transferred in this model for NATO is the authorization of force, not the obligation to use it. In other words, the U.S. government, or any other NATO member government, would seek authorization of NATO to use force, in the same way as they now must seek permission from the Security Council. (I discuss below the possibility of NATO and the Security Council disagreeing on the desirability of using force in any given situation.) But NATO should not have authority to demand that its member-states lend their armies for offensive use. As long as armies are staffed by nationals of particular states, the decision to put their lives at risk should remain in the hands of those states' governments. Building a NATO army separate from that of its member-states would be consistent with global democracy and might be a logical future development of NATO, but it would not be a necessary element of global democracy.

As long as other NATO members failed to invest in their own military capabilities (which stronger policies on burden sharing should help correct), the United States would retain a de facto veto right on offensive operations because other members would probably not be able to mount such operations without American military assets. But the majority vote for the use of force would provide other member-states with a de jure veto right on offensive operations proposed by the United States, provided that they mustered a majority of votes within NATO.

As a last resort, any member-state would retain the right to secede from NATO and act contrary to its decisions (feature 2). In contrast with what happens at the United Nations Security Council, where rules can be ignored and work can go on albeit with less credibility, global democracy is based on the rule of law. Second-tier intergovernmental organizations like NATO should include expulsion mechanisms for states that do not comply with their decisions. Seceding states would always be able to continue collaborating with NATO member-states in the framework of the United Nations and other first-tier organizations.

Secession would be a real option, but it would be a tough decision for any politician to make, as NATO membership would have over time brought about substantial defense dependencies vis-à-vis other member-states. Such dependencies would probably be very limited for the United States, thanks to its overwhelming military superiority. But even for an American president, leaving NATO, which would be tantamount to sinking it and creating a whole new and uncertain geopolitical environment, would be a very tough call. Nevertheless, I am now going to explore a "plan B," a defense alliance without the United States.

GLOBAL DEMOCRACY ASSUMES THAT international institutions would continue to evolve incrementally, and that several institutional experiments might occur at the same time. The various institutional reforms of NATO proposed above could occur over a long period of time and be sequenced in different ways. They could also occur in parallel with other institutional developments. In the next few paragraphs, I describe how the European Union could start playing a more assertive role in the global security policy area. It is in my mind a second-best scenario, first because European Union members lack many of the resources that NATO members have, and second because competition between several defense alliances could itself prove destabilizing, even though the membership of those defense alliances would significantly overlap. I nevertheless believe that the European Union could play a useful role in promoting global peace and security, and that European leadership could eventually induce the United States to embrace global democracy, rather than pulling the North Atlantic alliance apart.

The Europeans' military capacity to promote peace and security in the world is of course modest compared to that of the United States. That is partly due to a lack of vision for European defense. Here is such a vision. Defense could become the next policy area through which the Europeans could stabilize the world by strengthening the rule of law. The expansion of the European Union has been a big success for its new member-states, starting with Southern Europe, following with Central and Eastern Europe, and possibly culminating in some years with the membership of Turkey, which has already benefited from rapprochement with the European Union. But such expansion has claimed a social and economic toll on older member-states of North-Western Europe, in terms of trade competition, migration flows, and budgetary outlays. Turkey is therefore likely to wait a while before gaining the full prerogatives of membership, and it is hard to contemplate any expansion beyond the European continent (e.g., Maghreb, Middle East), not only because of cultural prejudices but perhaps primarily for economic reasons.

One way to continue spreading some of the benefits of European Union membership while minimizing the cost of expansion for existing members would be to offer flexible memberships, allowing states to join some corpus of European Union rules but not others. Such flexibility already exists, as some European Union members have been allowed to opt out of the monetary union and of border-control rules (the so-called Schengen area). Likewise, new member-states from other continents could be admitted in the Union provided that they opted out of the transfer budgets (e.g., the agricultural budget and regional development funds) and of the regulations regarding free movement of persons. In other words, they would only benefit from the free movement of goods and capital with European states, which would definitely not be as advantageous as full European Union membership, but would nevertheless be very attractive for many states.

A tighter European defense policy could be another area that some European Union member-states could embrace, but from which others could opt out. This is a proposal that has actually been seriously considered for a while and, despite the setback of the European constitution, might well happen within a decade. Opponents argue that any European defense policy would undermine NATO without adding much to it. But the idea proposed here is slightly different. The European Union's defense alliance would add something to NATO in that it would be open to countries located outside of the North Atlantic region. In a global democratic perspective, all states in the world would be entitled to join it, while being asked to opt out of some or all other policy areas of the European Union. The European Union's defense alliance (which, as a global organization, would require another name) would function in the same way as the expanded and reformed NATO I described above: secession right, restricted opt-out and veto rights, human rights entry test, free entry, majority voting with votes weighted by population, and independent judiciary. All these features are already enshrined in European law and practice, although extending such a thing as majority voting to the foreign policy and defense area would certainly be a big and difficult step for some member-states to take.

There are two big differences in the way the European Union's defense alliance and the expanded and reformed NATO proposed above would function. The first is that the former would not represent a credible dissuasion force in many parts of the world. The European Union's current capacity to defend, say, Malaysia is not good, to say the least. Membership in the European Union's defense alliance would therefore not be of much value to the Malaysians. It would also be dangerous for the Europeans, since their inability to defend Malaysia would damage the credibility of the whole alliance. It would therefore be prudent to amend the free entry policy, by selecting states that the European Union's defense alliance could actually defend.

The European Union could pacify large parts of Africa, for example.

France already has a number of bilateral defense treaties with African states, and has prepositioned military assets in the region. Some of these defense treaties could be turned into a Europe-based multilateral alliance according to the principles of global democracy. Britain has demonstrated both its capacity to intervene in Africa and the utility of such intervention in the case of Sierra Leone, which it pacified at little cost in 1999. In some cases, like Sierra Leone, the military challenge posed by disorganized and untrained rebel forces is quite manageable for European forces, and the benefits of intervention are tremendous. In other cases, like Somalia in the early 1990s, the military cost can be greater, although no one will ever know how many American soldiers would have lost their lives had U.S. armed forces pursued their mission to completion instead of fleeing after the first handful of casualties. Perhaps more importantly, though, the European Union's defense alliance would prevent conflicts through a dissuasion effect. A democracy like Mali, which is surrounded by states in the midst of civil unrest, could benefit tremendously from that dissuasion, at a fairly low cost for the European Union.

The second difference is that some European states would be members of two defense alliances, with different claims on the same military assets, and possibly conflicting policies to address particular crises. Tensions between the two alliances would unavoidably occur. Overt conflicts between the two should not occur because the members of the European Union defense alliance would be able to speak with one voice at NATO and veto any NATO policy or decision that would contradict European Union policy or decision. But the corollary of such veto would likely be unilateral action by the United States that could conflict with European action. Such conflict would decrease if the European Union's defense alliance focused on areas neglected by NATO, such as Africa. However, there would still be conflicting demands on military assets, as deployment of existing forces and investments in new types of military capacity would differ depending on each alliance's priorities.

The European Union's defense alliance, although lacking NATO's military might, would probably gain legitimacy thanks to its openness to the rest of the world and its democratic decision-making processes. Since legitimacy is often—though by no means always—as important and sometimes more important for resolving international crises than military might, the European Union's defense alliance could gain significant influence in world affairs, and, over time, induce the United States to embrace global democracy at NATO, which would eventually render the European Union's defense alliance redundant.

Many proponents of a stronger European defense policy advocate it—openly or not—in the spirit of strengthening Europe's "superpower" status in the world, to balance the existing "hyperpower" of the United States as well as the rising superpowers of Asia. That is also the main concern of opponents of a stronger European defense policy, who do not want a European superpower to oppose the United States. Global democracy embraces both these views by proposing the emergence of an inclusive superpower. Global democracy advocates that the European Union should cease to be exclusively European by opening its membership to the rest of the world in order to avoid a nationalist (or continentalist, in this case) foreign policy.

Global democracy actually represents a challenge to European foreign policy as much as to American foreign policy. Europeans are currently schizophrenic in their attitude toward foreign policy. Within Europe, they fully embrace global democracy. But toward the rest of the world, they are multilateralists. The commonality between these two approaches is the promotion of the rule of law: International affairs, like domestic policy, should be pursued in the framework of rules accepted by everyone. The rule of law is an important aspect of democracy, but is by no means all there is to democracy. Historically, the rule of law has preceded the emergence of democracy. Europeans behave in the same way as ancient Babylonian kings, the first rulers to forego arbitrary decisions in favor of laws, without actually sharing power. Europeans like rule-based multilateral forums like the Security Council or the World Trade Organization as long as they keep hoarding power in those bodies, allowing them to set policy for the rest of the world. Europeans need to take another step toward their ideal of rule-based global politics by shifting their model from Babylonian kings to Athenian democrats and actually sharing power with the people of the world.

How would global democracy help promote peace and security?

Now that I have sketched the global democratic approach to global peace and security policies in a couple scenarios, I will argue that such an approach would help make the world a safer place. I will base this argument on the first scenario only: expansion and reform of NATO.

In a nutshell, the advantage of NATO over the United Nations Security Council to police the world is that it is backed by credible military power. The Security Council has utterly failed in its mission to bring about world peace in the past sixty years, but not for lack of military power. After all, the five permanent members of the Security Council have combined armed forces that are mightier than the combined armed forces of NATO member-states. What the Security Council has sorely lacked is the credibility to use that power, which has in turn been due to disagreements over foreign policy and the veto power that each permanent member has on the others' preferred policies.

On the other hand, the disadvantage of NATO over the Security Council to police the world is that it is less legitimate, being an exclusive club of rich and powerful states. (I am actually quite critical of the Security Council's own legitimacy, but I must admit that it is perceived as more legitimate than NATO by many observers, especially in non-NATO countries.)

The bet of global democracy is thus that the incremental expansion of an organization like NATO could increase its legitimacy, as well as its military might, without decreasing its credibility. I am going to develop that proposition by considering how a would-be expanded and reformed NATO would be able to deal more effectively with the four main kinds of security threats: interstate wars, civil wars, the proliferation of weapons of mass destruction, and terrorism.

TO DEAL WITH INTERSTATE wars, an expanded and reformed NATO would add very significant value. Thanks to its credible deterrence, NATO could expand security and stability to large portions of the world. NATO has actually used its defense capacity only once, by supporting the American retaliation against Afghanistan in 2001. But the fact that this precedent is unique is actually a sign of very high credibility: No one had attacked NATO member-states before because of the fear of retaliation. However, expanding NATO might decrease the credibility of its deterrence. Nationals of existing NATO members would probably be less willing to die to protect nationals of new member-states, with whom they would have fewer cultural or historical ties. Nevertheless, this decrease in credibility would be fairly small if the expansion were progressive and involved only stable democracies. For it would be very costly for existing NATO members to renege on their obligation to defend new members.

To use an analogy, NATO membership is like a first-class plane ticket, while United Nations membership is like an economy-class ticket. As long as you remain in the exclusive first class, you do not have much incentive to care for those in economy class. Hence you do not care if the economy class gets downgraded: no meals, no leg space, and so on. That is what happened to the United Nations. Being themselves well protected, NATO members have not faced a strong incentive to maintain the Security Council's credibility. The global democratic approach to global security policy is to build a bigger first class and welcome all democratic states into it as a matter of policy. Although they would still be likely to neglect those states that remained in economy class, existing NATO members would not allow the arrival of new members to downgrade the first class because they would themselves have no where else to go. Expanding the first class would have costs, but that are costs that global democrats (as opposed to benevolent imperialists, nationalists, multilateralists, and localists) would be willing to pay in order to build a better, safer world. I will discuss shortly what these costs might be when I explore whether the institutional reforms proposed here fit the national interests of relevant states.

One could argue that decreasing the risk of interstate wars is a fine goal, but is not very relevant at a time when the real threats are the proliferation of weapons of mass destruction and terrorism. That is true from the perspective of existing NATO members, and even then only in the short and medium term. From a global perspective, interstate wars remain a very important threat. The liberation of Kuwait by allied forces in 1991, authorized by the United Nations, sent a strong signal that the international community would no longer tolerate the invasion and annexation of one sovereign state by another. However, that signal was not as strong as it appeared, since Kuwait and Iraq were geopolitically important states. Small states that are not particularly important to the United States and its allies have good reason to worry about interstate wars. Moreover, outright invasion and annexation is only the most severe kind of interstate war. Several border wars have erupted since 1991, including a very bloody one between Ethiopia and Eritrea in 1998–1999, which might break out again at any time and which continues to divert enormous resources away from the economic development of these two very poor countries. Another form of interstate war particularly relevant to African countries is the active support or benign neglect by one state of rebel groups wreaking havoc in a neighboring state. A variant of that is state-sponsored international terrorism (e.g., Iranian support of Palestinian terrorist groups or Afghan support of Al Qaida until 2001), which is very relevant to all countries, NATO members included.

Taking a longer view, the threat of interstate war is likely to increase significantly as powers like China, Japan, Russia, India, or Pakistan develop economically and flex their muscles militarily. In the long haul, the only way for the United States and its allies to avoid a nasty cold war with a rising China is, in my view, to demonstrate that they are ready to share power with China under the framework of democratic institutions, which is what global democracy is all about. As long as China would turn down an open invitation of NATO membership due in part to the human rights entry test, expanding NATO to countries like Thailand, Malaysia, or the Philippines could prove very important in stabilizing Asia.

An expanded and reformed NATO would also be able to, but would not be bound to, intervene in interstate wars between non-member-states. That is already the case today. As an offensive force, however, NATO is currently much less credible than as a deterrence force. Like the United Nations, NATO has been and would likely continue to be reluctant to assert itself and use force to restore peace outside of the territories of its member-states. It has used force offensively only two times in its history of more than forty years, with its interventions in Bosnia and Kosovo in the 1990s. Bosnia's intervention was in response to a call of the United Nations Security Council. The operation in Kosovo was not.

NATO's reluctance to intervene beyond its borders with, or especially without, Security Council authorization has been due mostly to a lack of altruism or incentives, as explained above with the airline analogy. But it has also been due to its legitimacy to do so being contested, both internally, as NATO's mission is formally confined to the North Atlantic area, and externally, as any NATO intervention without Security Council approval would involve diplomatic costs.

The expansion of NATO would increase its legitimacy, as it would incrementally become a truly global organization representing a large and diverse portion of the world population. That increase in legitimacy might increase NATO's proclivity to restore peace outside of its borders. For example, the first African members might urge other NATO members to intervene in conflicts between other African countries. Besides, more NATO interventions would be likely if NATO members including the United States were to commit not to intervene unilaterally, as I recommended above, because members that are now weary of interventionism would be pressured to take responsibility instead of ducking behind unilateral American interventions. Nevertheless, NATO would remain much less likely to defend non-member-states than member-states because of insufficient altruism or incentives. (Some non-member-states would anyway be governed by dictators who would not deserve being defended.)

A N EXPANDED AND REFORMED NATO would also be very helpful for the second type of threat—civil wars—mostly as a preventive instrument. It would be in the national interest of many states to pursue NATO membership. Because of the human rights entry test, these states would need to implement a series of reforms that would strengthen their ability to deal with internal conflicts peacefully, as exemplified by the case of Turkey and its accession process to the European Union. Once admitted to NATO, the human rights entry test and independent judiciary would further entrench these national institutions and decrease the risk of civil war, as demonstrated by the cases of Greece, Portugal, and Spain in the European Union. In the event that separatist terrorism or, less likely, a civil war would break out within a NATO member-state, the very existence of the human rights entry test would bolster that state's legitimacy to fight the insurrection, which is critical because legitimacy is always important, and sometimes decisive, in determining the winner of a civil war. The human rights entry test would also constrain a member-state's ability to fight the insurrection by restraining rules of engagement and making available courts to punish would-be war criminals, but that would be the price member-states would have to pay for the boost in legitimacy that NATO membership would generate. Member-states unwilling to pay that price would be free to leave the organization.

NATO should also be able to intervene militarily in non-member-states in order to end gross violations of human rights (e.g., genocide, crimes against humanity). After many years of controversy and several contested cases of "humanitarian interventions" (e.g., Somalia, Sierra Leone, Kosovo), the United Nations finally recognized the international community's responsibility to protect civilians in conflict situations, including through the use of force, at its 2005 World Summit.[2] The responsibility to protect is a notion that is certainly compatible with global democracy, which promotes a world where all people enjoy human rights. The International Commission on Intervention and State Sovereignty, an independent panel of experts set up by the Canadian government, has come up with a policy proposal to apply the responsibility to protect. It consists of six conditions to trigger humanitarian military interventions:

- *Right authority*: The Security Council is the sole authority to pass judgment on whether the conditions are met.
- *Just cause*: The humanitarian crimes ought to be sufficiently serious to warrant military intervention; the threshold is discussed in some detail in the report.
- *Right intention*: The intervention ought to be motivated by the humanitarian circumstances (although, the commission adds, mixed motives cannot be avoided).
- *Last resort*: The intervention ought to take place after reasonable efforts to prevent the humanitarian crimes from taking place.
- *Proportional means*: The intervention should not go beyond redressing the humanitarian crimes. It should of course respect the laws of war.

- *Reasonable prospects*: The intervention must have a good chance of success. It should not trigger collateral casualties worse than the atrocities that it aimed at preventing in the first place.[3]

Given the Security Council's record of shunning humanitarianism based on the geopolitical interests of its permanent members, I would challenge the commission's first condition. The Security Council rightfully refused to authorize the interventions in Kosovo in 1999,[4] and accepted to authorize well-founded interventions in Somalia in 1994 and Sierra Leone in 2000, but it failed to authorize interventions in numerous other cases where it would have been justified, including in Rwanda in 1994, in the Congo since the mid-1990s, and in Sudan since 2004. Haiti in 1994 was a rare case of interventions that the Security Council did authorize but that was not justified according to the International Commission on Intervention and State Sovereignty's conditions. On the other hand, bypassing the Security Council and allowing self-appointed big powers to launch humanitarian intervention by their own authority would certainly lead to abuses, such as claims of humanitarianism in the cases of Kosovo or even Iraq in 2003 testify. (Iraq was a totalitarian state that had committed atrocities in the past but was not slaughtering its citizens by the thousands in 2003.)

Under a global democratic approach, the condition of right authority would entrust the authority to trigger humanitarian military interventions onto two organs, not just one. One of these organs ought to be a court, composed of independent, life-appointed judges (feature 9 of global democracy). Their independence would add assurance that the conditions of just cause, right intention, last resort, and proportional means would be met. Politicians are not to be trusted to make such judgments, as they are bound to be influenced by their constituencies' interests, as the experience with humanitarian interventions so far has demonstrated. The other organ ought to consist of elected politicians, advised by military personnel, because judges should not be expected to pass judgment on the condition of reasonable prospects. The International Criminal Court and the Security Council might respectively fulfill these roles, provided that the former were also given the prerogative of independent initiative (at the time being, the International Criminal

Court may only prosecute cases initiated either by its member-states for violations perpetrated against their nationals or on their territories, or by the Security Council). In a global democratic perspective, the council of an expanded and reformed NATO and a new judicial organ of NATO could take on these roles instead, and supersede the authority of the Security Council.

Such an institutional setup would significantly reduce the risk that self-interested politicians would pervert the International Commission on Intervention and State Sovereignty's fine policy proposal. It would by no means eliminate that risk, however, as politicians could invoke the condition of reasonable prospects in bad faith in order to avoid an intervention that they were not ready to make based on less laudable grounds. Nevertheless, pronouncements by an independent judiciary that gross human rights violations warranting military intervention occurred would put a welcome and significant pressure on politicians. However, a side effect of independent initiative by the court would be the potential to trigger unmanageable conflicts, as governments that felt threatened by court action might be led to take preemptive military actions. For that reason, the Security Council, or NATO's council, ought to have the right to veto the court's jurisdiction over a specific list of states on the ground of serious security threat. Such an exception would be consistent with the principle of reasonable prospect, and it would be difficult to abuse: It would be hard for NATO politicians to claim that Sudan posed a serious security threat to NATO member-states, for instance.

B Y CONTRAST WITH ITS potential impact on interstate wars and civil wars, the effects of global democracy on the fight against the proliferation of weapons of mass destruction and against international terrorism would likely be small. The key task with regard to proliferation is to increase control mechanisms of the Non-Proliferation Treaty, the Chemical Weapons Convention, and the Biological Weapons Convention. Free entry in NATO would make that easier, as states would trade their right to develop weapons of mass destruction against a strong security guarantee, including the American nuclear deterrent. The Non-Proliferation Treaty already obligates the five official nuclear powers to protect the other signatories, but that commitment is not nearly as credible as

NATO membership would be. That said, this advantage should not be overstated because the states that are currently most willing to become nuclear powers are also those least likely to pursue NATO membership in the foreseeable future. Nevertheless, NATO's adoption of a free entry policy would itself represent a peaceful overture that would bear on the decisions of would-be nuclear powers in a constructive way. And it would probably encourage other states—those that are neither current NATO members nor considering building weapons of mass destruction at this time—to support tighter control mechanisms more earnestly.

From the perspective of existing and new NATO members, global democracy would offer essentially the same options to deal with would-be nuclear powers as those that are available to them today: carrots such as trade treaties and aid, and sticks such as trade sanctions and even the possibility of preemptive attacks. The only difference—an important one—would be that member-states of an expanded and reformed NATO would pursue the same policy decided through majority voting with votes weighted by population.

A global democratic approach to international terrorism would also include the same options as those that are available today. Most of the work to fight terrorism should continue to be a matter of national law enforcement, and most of the debate about restricting civil liberties for the sake of increasing security should continue to happen at the national level as well. Options for international cooperation are and would continue to include international exchange of intelligence between law enforcement agencies, international cooperation on covert operations, and international judicial agreements on arrest warrants, extraditions, and the like. Military attacks against terrorist havens, which I considered above as a form of interstate war, would also remain an option. The prospect of NATO membership might induce some states to participate more zealously in such international cooperation. But that advantage is actually small because most states are already cooperating pretty well in the fight against terrorism, and those that are not would be unlikely to seek NATO membership in the foreseeable future were NATO to adopt a free entry policy.

G LOBAL DEMOCRACY WOULD ALSO have two general effects on policies addressing any of the four kinds of security threats mentioned
above: It would enhance their coherence as well as their legitimacy. Under current international institutions where veto and opt-out rights prevail, allies can undermine each other's policies when they disagree on a
particular course of action.

A typical example of such a situation is when allies adopt different
stances toward a common threat, such as Europeans trying to placate
Iran to denuclearize it and the Chinese similarly trying to placate North
Korea while the United States favors a more coercive approach to both.
The bellicose American rhetoric vis-à-vis both states does not help the
Europeans and Chinese persuade the Iranians and North Koreans that
they do not need nuclear weapons. And the veto Europeans wield at
the Security Council to block tough sanctions or military intervention
against Iran, or the aid the Chinese give to the North Koreans, does not
help the Americans convey a sense of urgency on the nuclear proliferation issue. In both cases, the U.S. government seems content with the
diplomatic efforts of its allies for now. But one can reasonably anticipate
that the patience of the United States will run short faster than that of
the Europeans and Chinese, or that the sticks Americans will propose
once everyone agrees that the diplomatic route has run its course will go
beyond what the Europeans and Chinese will feel comfortable with. At
that point, multilateralism will become stalled. Benevolent imperialists
will be right to condemn the ensuing paralysis as dangerous. And they
will urge the United States to take matters in its own hands, ignoring
international institutions and some allies at the risk of losing some international legitimacy—regardless of the dire consequences that lack of
legitimacy can have. Despite the Iraqi quagmire, a unilateral attack by
the United States against Iran remains a possibility. And it would result
in the same problems as the Iraqi situation generated: deeper loss of credibility of the United Nations, transatlantic rift, more anti-Americanism
throughout the world. Hawks may win but they would again be bruised,
and America would pay a higher price for disarming Iran than it would
otherwise have.

By contrast, a global democratic approach would combine the benevolent imperialists' decisiveness and credibility with the multilateralists'

legitimacy. Members of the enlarged and reformed NATO would jointly and democratically decide on one course of action, and then assume collective responsibility for whatever decision had been reached, just as opposition parties assume responsibility for their government's foreign policies even if they criticize them. NATO's decisions could be a compromise solution including a mix of carrots and sticks, but the decisions would be applied coherently in the framework of a single plan of action.

Just as national democracies do not need to be weak and irresolute, as demonstrated by a United States that does not hesitate to use force, intergovernmental organizations need not be wavering either, provided that they make decisions without veto or opt-out rights. Decisiveness does not come at the expense of open debate in national democracies, and it should be so at the global level of government as well. Disagreements will continue to occur, both among nationals of the same state and between national governments. Global democracy is agnostic about how hard or soft an approach is best to deal with security threats. Global democrats can be hawkish or dovish. However, global democracy does require that decisions between these approaches be made by a majority of all citizens, on the grounds that they are all affected by these decisions and that human beings are all equal. Military decisions ought not be made by the citizens of the United States alone on the ground that their government is the most powerful militarily.

With that in mind, it is hard to anticipate the policy direction a reformed and expanded NATO would be likely to take, whether bellicose or pacifist. The German Marshall Fund of the United States conducts annual opinion polls in America and Europe on security issues.[5] Despite the transatlantic schism over Iraq, it appears that opinions largely converge. Both Americans and Europeans strongly support multilateralism and the United Nations, although the former are noticeably readier to defy the United Nations when vital interests are at stake. A majority of Americans support initiatives championed by Europeans but opposed by the Bush administration such as the Kyoto Protocol and the International Criminal Court. Both have roughly the same assessment of threats. But they differ in their preferred response to threats: Europeans are more inclined to use diplomacy and economic incentives and sanctions and less inclined to use force than the Americans. However, this difference in general opinion can hide convergence in particular crisis situations. The Iraq crisis of 2003 was of course the best example of divergence, with a majority of Americans and British initially supporting the war, contrary to the public opinions of most other NATO countries. But there has been a convergence since the height of the diplomatic fallout: A majority of Americans now believe that the war was a mistake and increased the terrorist threat, while a majority of French, Germans, and Spaniards would be ready to dispatch troops in Iraq in the framework of a United Nations mission. On Iran, which is probably going to pose the next big challenge to transatlantic unity, opinions in 2006 were remarkably similar. Thirty-five percent of Americans and thirty-eight percent of Europeans would accept a nuclear Iran if diplomatic efforts failed. Forty-five percent of Americans and thirty-seven percent of Europeans would support military action (the rest being undecided).

Opinions are of course not monolithic. Sharp divergences exist across European countries and between Republicans and Democrats in America. Europeans are better aligned with Republicans on some issues, such as the balance between security and civil liberties and the promotion of democracy abroad, and with the Democrats on others, such as the support for multilateralism and restraint in the use of force. Another poll carried out by the Chicago Council on Foreign Relations in the United States in 2004 compares the opinions of policy elites with those of the general public.[6] It appears that both the public and the elite—with the exception of Congressional Republicans—support multilateralism and fairly altruistic foreign policies, but policy elites tend to believe that the public is less altruistic than it actually is. A related study by the Aspen Institute reveals the existence of a "looking glass syndrome," by which the press and decision makers look at each other to guess where the public stands on foreign policy, without actually consulting the public.[7]

All these data pertain to Europeans and Americans only. Were NATO to expand on new continents, the attitudes of the "median NATO voter" would be likely to change. That voter's attitudes about an international security crisis in a particular region would also depend on the number of NATO member-states in that region. Surely, NATO's approach to a crisis in South Asia would be heavily influenced by India's membership, for instance. Through expansion, NATO would thus incorporate more diverse perspectives on, and better regional knowledge of, crises, which should make for better informed debates and therefore more balanced and fair policies.

However, even as NATO expands, some states would remain outside of it, and just as every national foreign policy is loaded with prejudice, so would be NATO's foreign policy. Even if, say, India's membership would bring a better understanding of a crisis in South Asia, it would also bring some of the prejudices that Indians have vis-à-vis their neighbors. NATO's foreign policy, however democratic it might be, would therefore remain vulnerable to the criticism I developed against benevolent imperialism in particular: the lack of adequate check-and-balance mechanisms to protect foreigners, in this case, nationals of non-NATO members.

Like the United States, a reformed and enlarged NATO might commit serious human rights violations as a result of poor feedback mechanisms from nationals of non-NATO countries. I nevertheless believe that that would be less likely thanks to the greater diversity of attitudes on international affairs among NATO voters compared to the diversity of attitudes among American voters alone. If a NATO policy did turn out to seriously violate the human rights of nationals of non-NATO countries, such a story would have a greater chance of being picked up by the press of some NATO members, and then relayed by elected officials, which would then make it harder for officials of other NATO members to ignore. Currently, if the Indian press criticizes a foreign policy of the U.S. government, the Indian government will be unlikely to relay the criticism very strongly, even if it agrees with it, in order to maintain good diplomatic relations. Even if it did relay the criticism strongly, the U.S. government would likely ignore it. If India were part of NATO, the Indian government would be more likely to relay the criticism, firstly because it would share responsibility for the NATO policy, and secondly because it would have the voting power to influence the position of the U.S. government. Only if the positions of all major NATO member-states became well aligned (that is, only if diversity of opinion within NATO declined) would NATO become susceptible of abusing its power.

The United Nations Security Council—a first-tier intergovernmental organization in global democracy's framework—could be construed as a useful check on the power of the enlarged and reformed NATO. Since a

NATO intervention would automatically have the votes of three of the five permanent members (i.e., the United States, Britain, and France), and possibly votes of some nonpermanent members, and since a blocking coalition of seven nonpermanent members has been and would always continue to be very difficult to form, the question really comes down to whether China or Russia should be allowed to block NATO's military interventions. As long as NATO remained an exclusive club of Western powers, I would personally be wary of seeing it circumvent the Security Council (although a case could be made to do so to protect civilians in Darfur, for instance). But as NATO enlarged to an increasing number of countries and democratized its decision-making processes, it would progressively gain legitimacy and should feel increasingly free to override formal Chinese and Russian vetoes. Global democracy would then turn the Security Council from a decision-making body into a consultative body—even if that means violating Chapter VII of the United Nations Charter. That chapter has already been undermined by the wars of Kosovo and Iraq anyway, and it has otherwise not been used much despite of a large number of occasions when it probably should have been used.

Although China and Russia would add useful perspectives to NATO's debate, they would also, like every state, have vested interests in international disputes that could be detrimental to reaching just settlements. Even though China's (but not Russia's) demographic weight would justify its veto right from a majority-voting perspective, compared to the combined demographic weight of existing NATO members, majority voting is a necessary but not sufficient component of global democracy. If China or Russia were willing to comply with NATO's rules, they would be free to join the organization and get their fair share of power based on their respective demographic weight. That option is the most important difference between global democracy and benevolent imperialism: A reformed and enlarged NATO, unlike the United States, would be an inclusive power.

What political forces could bring about global democracy?

After having sketched what the global democratic approach to global peace and security could be and what difference it would make in the world, based on the scenario of an enlarged and reformed NATO, I am now going to muse on the long-term political feasibility of that scenario. I start by considering whether it would be in the interest of the main protagonists: the United States, other existing NATO members, and would-be new members.

From the perspective of the United States, NATO's expansion would have both costs and benefits. The cost would obviously be a loss of flexibility and control in managing global security. The United States is already bound by bilateral treaties, outside of NATO, to defend a small number of states: Australia, Japan, South Korea, New Zealand, and the Philippines. But the United States also has "status-of-forces" agreements with over a hundred states. These agreements stipulate conditions under which American military personnel may operate in a host state. They often come with implicit security guarantees for the host state or even for the government in place. For some states, such as Israel, that guarantee is as strong as the NATO treaty. Dealing bilaterally with these hundred states provides maximum flexibility to the U.S. government to minimize its commitments while maximizing the security of U.S. nationals, as each agreement can be tailor-made and reneged when circumstances change.

The benefit of the expansion of NATO for the United States would be increased deterrence. The drawback of flexibility is indeed that it undermines the credibility of deterrence. If some states currently having status-of-forces agreements with the United States were to join NATO, that would significantly increase dissuasion and therefore decrease the likelihood that the United States would ever have to actually use force to defend them. In that sense, the United States would be interested in extending NATO membership particularly to states that it means to defend anyway because of their geopolitical importance.

Besides expansion of the defense alliance, the scenario sketched above also proposed that NATO would probably play a more assertive role outside of its borders. Again, the United States would lose flexibility and control in managing global security if NATO took on more leadership. In particular, Americans would have a very hard time, to say the least, accepting that global security policy would be set democratically by all NATO members. On the other hand, the United States would benefit from burden sharing. Sharing power would also mean sharing responsibility, and other NATO members would likely become more willing to invest in defense (which could even become a legally binding commitment) and to commit their own troops in crisis situations. Despite the United States' tremendous military superiority, the current situation in Iraq and Afghanistan demonstrates that burden sharing remains important. American public opinion also consistently supports it.

On balance, the objective long-term cost of sharing power is not necessarily greater than the long-term benefits of greater dissuasion and burden sharing. However, it is certain that no mainstream American politicians would endorse the endgame of global democracy at this time: Nationalists would easily rouse the electorate against them. It would obviously take a lot of advocacy effort over several decades to persuade Americans that global democracy was the right way forward. Nevertheless, it is not necessary for Americans to endorse the endgame of global democracy before they start taking small steps toward it. Modest reforms such as integrating Mexico into NATO—assuming Mexico were willing to join—would not seem completely unrealistic even today. And in the long term, when the Iraq quagmire eventually wanes from Americans' memories, it is likely to be harder for future presidents of the United States to declare triumphantly that "America will never seek a permission slip to defend the security of our country." For, in the long term, America is unlikely to be able to carry the burden of global security alone, despite its current overwhelming military might, and legitimacy is likely to play an increasingly important role in international crises.

From the point of view of other existing NATO members, NATO's expansion would dilute their privileged status as primary allies of the United States. Militarily, the power brought by new members might not compensate for the new threats faced by the alliance as a whole. That situation would lead either to a loss of credibility of the alliance as a whole, or to higher defense spending by all members. Politically, NATO's membership provides diplomatic clout relative to the rest of the world.

When this privilege becomes widely shared, its value is reduced. On the other hand, Europeans are more familiar with and receptive to the concept of global democracy presented here, and they would welcome a better-structured forum to set global security policy, particularly one in which they would themselves exercise significant influence.

As to letting NATO play a bigger role outside of its borders, Europeans would probably be divided. Some European Union member-states are not members of NATO to start with, precisely because they do not want to be involved in global policing. I have noted that worries of military overreach are greater in Europe than in the United States. However, such worries are in my view partially warranted because of the current lack of legitimacy of NATO, or even of a would-be European superpower, as a global cop. Europeans could become emboldened if either NATO or the European Union itself embraced the global democratic vision of global security policy that I have sketched. If that were accompanied by greater investments in defense, the democratization of NATO would become easier because the United States and Europeans would be more equal partners. Besides, I have noted that Europeans are as concerned about security as Americans. They have already moved beyond their traditional peacekeeping role to take on a major combat assignment in Afghanistan.[8]

Europeans are, overall, supportive of NATO, and the global democratic reforms I have proposed would on balance be likely to increase that support. The important issue that they need to figure out is whether they want to proactively push for such development, including perhaps creating a common European defense policy like the scenario I sketched. Europeans must decide how much they care about spreading their model of supranational law to stabilize the world.

Finally, from the point of view of potential new members, that is, democratic states that are not currently NATO members, a free-entry policy of NATO could only be a good thing, as they would gain an opportunity that is currently denied to them. That does not necessarily mean that they would seize it, though. Past American imperialism might make many Latin American countries think twice before applying. But that is largely because NATO has been an exclusive club so far, despite recent efforts of global partnerships, and the option of Latin American membership has never been seriously advanced. For Latin Americans, benefits of NATO membership would include (1) greater say in global security matters, which interests at least the largest states; (2) prevention of interstate wars, such as the border clashes between Peru and Ecuador in 1995, although such wars are arguably already quite unlikely; and, perhaps more importantly, (3) the strengthening of democratic institutions because of the human rights entry test. The entry test would constrain the way national governments would be able to deal with civil unrest, but adhering to it would also strengthen the governments' legitimacy and possibly even allow them to leverage NATO resources to mediate, arbitrate, contain, or suppress insurrections. Latin American states might also benefit economically from NATO membership, as financial markets might regard membership as a sign of political stability. Besides the constraints of the human rights entry test, the costs of NATO membership would include commitments of defense spending and greater expectations to participate in peacekeeping missions.

Similar costs and benefits would accrue to new African and Asian NATO members. For small and medium-sized Asian states like Cambodia, Malaysia, the Philippines, and Thailand, NATO membership could prove a very valuable protection when China, India, Japan, and Russia flex their military and economic muscles in the decades to come.

On the African continent, conflicts remain a major scourge that, together with HIV-AIDS and corruption, not only kill people but also prevent economic development. A study shows that peacekeeping operations are one of the most cost-effective forms of foreign aid.[9] If the conflict prevention impact of NATO dissuasion for would-be African member-states were added, cost effectiveness would be greater still. Most African conflicts are internal to a state, but most internal conflicts actually do destabilize neighboring states to some extent, through flows of refugees and black markets of weapons and raw materials, but also through cross-border raids of rebels or armies. Such cross-border raids and traffic would be much more dangerous for rebel groups if they were perpetrated within the territory of a NATO member-state, as this would justify a full-fledged NATO campaign against the rebel group in question, and possibly against any neighboring state supporting that rebel group.

The human rights entry test would also strengthen the institutions of African NATO members to deal more effectively with their own internal conflicts and prevent them from escalating into armed conflicts. Although only the most stable African states would be able to meet the conditions for NATO membership in the foreseeable future, neighboring states could benefit as well, as humanitarian interventions in failed states would become more likely. Not only could African NATO members better advocate for humanitarian interventions in Africa, but it would actually be in NATO's interest to contain some African conflicts before they seriously threaten African NATO members.

N OW THAT I HAVE reviewed national interests in the global democratic approach to global security policy, it is also worth considering transnational interests. I noted in the introduction that three political forces are likely to converge to support global democracy in the coming decades: the global movement for social justice; the rising "middle class" of populous poor and middle-income countries like Brazil, China and India; and the global elite that supports civil and political rights in general and would be willing to reform globalization in order to preserve it from a return to the dark ages of nationalism. While these forces are already discernible in the area of global economic policy, they are much less apparent in the global security policy area. That is not to say that they could not start developing in the near future. They have good reasons to do so.

Populous poor and middle-income countries like Bangladesh, Brazil, India, and Nigeria have already demonstrated a willingness to participate in global security policy by lending significant numbers of peacekeeping troops to United Nations operations. However, they have not started to challenge the current multilateral policy-making framework. Instead, the biggest among them, such as India, mostly seek to increase their formal power within the existing United Nations institutions, primarily by securing a permanent seat on the Security Council. While permanent seats for additional poor and middle-income countries would be very welcome, they would not significantly change the balance of power in the council unless they also obtained veto rights, in which case what they would bring to the council in terms of legitimacy would be more than compensated by a further loss in decisiveness, effectiveness, and hence credibility. Russia and China are of course middle-income powers that already benefit from the veto right at the Security Council. They use it at times constructively to balance the power of the United States and Europeans. However, like the other permanent members, they can also be obstructionist for less laudable reasons, from fear of domestic opposition to protection of domestic economic interests. The veto right is just not the solution to the global challenge of securing peace in the world.

One of the reasons poor and middle-income powers are stuck with current multilateralism is simply a lack of imagination. The end of the Cold War and the triumph of global capitalism led to the "governance without government" paradigm, which, although flawed, rejuvenated multilateralism for two decades and allowed scholars and practitioners alike to think outside of the box about global economic, human rights, and environmental policy. In the global security policy area, by contrast, the main ideas that the end of the Cold War engendered were the "end of history" and the "clash of civilizations."[10] The former started to popularize benevolent imperialism and its idea of a community of democracies, and the latter refurbished nationalism for a new era. Neither helped multilateralism out of its contradictions and stalemates on security issues. Neither presented rising poor and middle-income powers with constructive insights to contribute to world peace. By presenting a fresh new approach to global security policy, this book may offer food for thought to leaders of these rising powers—which would have little to lose and the most to gain from global democracy.

Global civil society has been very proactive in shaping global economic, human rights, and environmental policies since the end of the Cold War. The contrast with global security policy is stark. Perhaps in an attempt to stay clear of the moral dilemmas that questions of war and peace entail, the global movement for social justice has essentially surrendered the whole field of global security policy to nationalist and benevolent-imperialist think tanks.

The first Gulf War, the Kosovo war, and the Afghanistan war led many protesters to the streets, but one could not speak of a structured and proactive peace movement. Protesters rose in great numbers when the first bullet was fired—that is, when it was too late—and got back home when the heavy fighting was over. The ongoing war in Iraq—because of both its duration and relatively high number of American casualties—has generated a forceful and sustained movement that has had an impact in the 2006 Congressional elections in the United States. However, that movement does not have a vision for world peace beyond immediate withdrawal of American troops from Iraq—a policy that, in my opinion, could lead to greater chaos in Iraq without by itself reducing the virulence of international terrorism or taming the "clash of civilization" between the West and Islam.

The peace movement does not have the structure, continuity, and long-term vision that global nongovernmental organizations such as Amnesty International, Oxfam, or Greenpeace provide respectively to the human rights, development, and environmental movements. These and other mainstream organizations have taken a narrow view of global security policy, limiting themselves to disarmament (e.g., the ban on land mines won in 1998, current attempts to control trade in small arms, advocacy for nuclear disarmament), and to enforcement of international humanitarian law to protect civilians when wars do break out. They avoid endorsing or condemning the use of force to deal with particular crises, or they do so reactively from the narrow perspective of immediate protection of civilians, leaving longer-term considerations to politicians. It is definitely better than no involvement at all, but it does not amount to a viable strategy to achieve world peace.

At the time of writing, the United States and Iran are noticeably on a war path. The depth of the Iraq quagmire has reduced the chance of action during the Bush administration—though the most radical elements of that administration remain a source of concern—but this situation will not last forever and a new administration may find new political resolve to act. The United Nations Security Council has taken a first hostile step, in the form of limited sanctions. Yet the voice of the global movement for social justice on the issue is almost inaudible. Not only European governments, but also peace groups that support nuclear disarmament have endorsed the central premise of nationalists and benevolent imperialists: It is unacceptable for Iran to get the bomb. It is hard to find any dissenting voice in the mainstream press in America or Europe. When sanctions prove ineffective—which they are likely to, as Iran seems determined—the patience of nationalists and benevolent imperialists will run short. European governments as well as civil society groups that oppose the use of force will then find themselves hard pressed to say that, after all, it would not be the end of the world if Iran got the bomb. It would be too late for them to move a public opinion fed for several years on the premise of nationalists and benevolent imperialists.

I believe it would be wiser to impose reasonable sanctions against Iran to restrict its access to foreign nuclear technology and increase the price it pays for acquiring nuclear weapons, but otherwise to accept the notion that Iran would eventually acquire them. Once Iran did get the bomb, it would become wiser to treat Iran as an official nuclear power, along with Israel as well as India and Pakistan. It would be wiser to start a dialogue of deterrence with Iran, but at the same time engage in a peaceful dialogue between civilizations to decrease the tension and address the root causes that led Iran to seek the bomb in the first place. Such dual dialogue of deterrence and engagement is possible, as President Reagan and Secretary General Gorbachev demonstrated in the late 1980s. The only viable alternative to this course of action would be, in my view, disarmament of Iran through invasion and regime change, which I believe would have disastrous consequences in terms of fostering terrorism, nationalism, and further wars.

I expose my views on this subject only to illustrate the kind of conversations that progressive civil society groups would have at this time if they wanted to lead global security policy. Instead, such conversations (or rather, similar conversations with quite different conclusions) only occur within nationalist and benevolent-imperialist circles. That is of great concern to me. Indeed, it is one of the main reasons that temper my optimism about the development of global democracy. For global security policy drives international relations and determines the future of globalization, not global economic policy. I can nevertheless observe a growing realization among nongovernmental organizations that progress achieved on the economic front over the past couple of decades could be reversed by increased global insecurity. That gives me hope that global civil society would penetrate the security area more proactively and demand global democracy there, too.

The third political force that could eventually push for global democracy is the transnational elite of politicians, civil servants, and businesspeople who defend globalization. I have noted that European elites in particular could be opened to the global democratic approach to global security policy, primarily as a way to further the European project of stabilizing the world through the rule of law. While the potential exists in Europe, it would be unlikely to manifest itself unless both rising middle-income powers and global civil society exercise moral pressure on the elites to share power. Overall, global democracy is therefore likely to develop more slowly in the global security policy area. Its main driver is likely to be faster development of global democracy in the other policy areas, to which I now turn.

To CONCLUDE, THE GLOBAL democratic approach to global peace and security policy can perhaps best be described as extending peace and security to all democratic states by sharing the dissuasive power of Western military might in the framework of a defense alliance. This would be more credible than the security guarantees offered by the United Nations and by status-of-force agreements with the United States alone. In that sense, global democracy would primarily promote global peace and security in a quiet, preventive way.

Nevertheless, I have also explained how military power could actually be used according to global democracy. It is useful in that regard to contrast global democracy with benevolent imperialism, which also seeks to extend peace and security to all democratic states through Western military might. While the balance of military power among states, the threats perceived by each state, the options available to deal with these threats, and the attitudes of each state's public opinion about those options could all remain unchanged, what global democracy would change are the relationships between the following:

- The American empire and its main vassals, that is, states with which the United States currently has a defense treaty. Main vassals already enjoy the right of being protected by the United States, but they would gain more voice in shaping global security policy in exchange for burden sharing, that is, investing more in their own and in the world's defense.
- The American empire and its fringe vassals, that is, allied states (or

at least those with democratic institutions) that do not currently
have a defense treaty with the United States. Fringe vassals would
benefit greatly both from increased security and stability and from
increased influence. They would gain both rights and voice. But
they would also need to share the burden of collective defense.

- The American empire and its "strategic competitors," that is, its
potential enemies like China and Russia today but also perhaps
Japan and India in the distant future. Strategic competitors would
gain the option of cooperating on fair terms, that is, based on
a democratic sharing of power, rather than competing with the
United States. Even if strategic competitors chose not to seize that
option to start with, the fact that it would be available to them
would positively influence international relations by decreasing
defensiveness on their part. If they chose to join the global
democratic club, these strategic competitors would gain rights
of protection and would, by virtue of their demographic weight,
preserve or enhance the voice they already have by virtue of their
geopolitical weight.

- The American empire and its declared enemies, that is, Iran, North
Korea, and other states sponsoring terrorism. This relationship
would be handled by the United States and its allies based on
democratic decision making. For each case, they would jointly
adopt either a containment or engagement policy, global democracy
being agnostic about which is best in general.

In a nutshell, the essence of the global democratic approach to global
security is to build an inclusive superpower, one characterized by free
entry for all states meeting a minimum human rights entry test and by
a fair distribution of decision-making power (and fair sharing of defense
spending).

14

Promotion of Civil and Political Rights

THE VERY IDEA OF global democracy is to create new civil and political rights to ensure citizens control the public policies that are decided at the global level of government. Establishing direct legal relationships between citizens and their global government, unmediated by states, is an intrinsic part of the cosmopolitan democracy paradigm (see Chapter 3).[11]

Strictly speaking, however, global democracy could develop without new rights for citizens themselves. Most intergovernmental organizations have recourse procedures, and some have judicial or quasi-judicial bodies, allowing member-states to bring complaints against their decisions on behalf of their citizens. Such procedures can be construed as alternatives to the civil right of citizens to sue their global government directly. Likewise, representation by national government officials in intergovernmental organizations can be construed as an alternative to the political right of citizens to elect their global government representatives directly. In democracies, the executive branch of national government is either directly or indirectly elected by the people, and can therefore legitimately make decisions on global public policies in their name. The only reforms to current intergovernmental organizations that are needed to advance global democracy are the nine features presented in Chapter 12, including weighing the votes of national representatives by population (feature 7) to replace the "one state, one vote" decision-making rule, and a human rights entry test to ensure that government officials casting their state's vote are indeed representative of their people (feature 5).

Nevertheless, creating new civil and political rights for citizens, as opposed to merely leveling the playing field among states, would be highly desirable. The ability for people and companies to sue their global government directly would be much more empowering than their current ability to lobby their national government to bring about a complaint on their behalf. National officials face many competing demands, and political considerations on their part can easily get in the way of justice. It is much easier for European companies to bring a case to the European Court of Justice as plaintiffs in their own right than it is for companies to persuade their governments to introduce a complaint before the World Trade Organization's Dispute Settlement Body. Governments of poor and middle-income countries are reluctant to bring complaints against the United States or the European Union for diplomatic reasons. Moreover, the European Court of Justice's decisions are binding upon member-states in pretty much the same way as their national courts' decisions. By contrast, the Dispute Settlement Body merely authorizes states that win a case to impose retaliatory measures against states that have harmed them with improper commercial practices. It is often not in the interest of poor and middle-income countries to actually carry out such punitive measures against the United States or the European Union, as it can harm their own companies that depend on American or European imports.

Several intergovernmental organizations already offer the opportunity for citizens to bring grievances to independent judicial or quasi-judicial panels in their own right, typically after they have exhausted all recourses in national law. For example, several United Nations human rights treaties offer complaint procedures that individuals or private organizations can bring against states. Although states can ignore with impunity the ensuing recommendations of the recourse bodies, such recommendations can be politically useful to embarrass governments that commit human rights violations. The Council of Europe's European Court of Human Rights is perhaps the best example of an international court allowing individuals to sue governments for human rights abuses. Its verdicts are binding for the Council of Europe's members-states. Examples of global judicial or quasi-judicial bodies accessible by citizens in other policy areas include the Independent Panel of the World Bank, which considers complaints about negative impacts of World Bank projects. The International Criminal Court is a good example of an international court able to indict individuals for gross human rights violations and sentence and imprison them. Such mechanisms should be strengthened to make global democracy more robust.

To foster the political right of representation, creating directly elected parliaments within intergovernmental organizations would be desirable for a couple of reasons. First, international boundaries sometimes represent odd constituencies to aggregate individuals' preferences about global public policies. For example, farmers in India and China probably share more common interests on many economic issues than they do with city dwellers of their respective countries. It would make sense for them to be able to vote as a block against city dwellers, something that would not be possible if each state could cast only one vote (even if that vote were weighted by the state's population). By contrast, if each state could send a number of representatives to the parliament of an intergovernmental organization, some representatives would presumably be able to represent rural interests, and others, urban interests.

Second, representatives to intergovernmental organizations would be more accountable to citizens if they were directly elected than if they continued to be appointed by national governments, even if those governments would themselves be directly or indirectly elected. National governments would always remain accountable to their electorates primarily for their national policies because global policies would continue to represent a smaller proportion of the decisions they make. Hence, it would be hard for national electorates to sanction national governments for their wrong-headed global policies as long as they remained fairly satisfied with their governments' national policies.

Direct elections of representatives to intergovernmental organizations would also be likely to improve citizens' access to decision makers. The political process would become more transparent because citizens would more readily know who is in charge of what policies and parliamentarians would be more likely than political appointees to meet their constituents and answer their questions. Periodic elections, rather than arcane closed-door negotiating forums among diplomats, would be regular occasions for broad-based debates on important global public policy issues. In the European Union, some national parliaments (e.g., the Danish Folketing) have done a better job than others at holding their government officials accountable for the decisions they make at the European Council. Nevertheless, most people believe the European Parliament has a role to play to close the gap between the Union and its citizens.

Each second-tier intergovernmental organization could have its own parliament. That would multiply the number of elections, which could be costly and increase voter apathy as voters could be confused by the large number of organizations. But cost could be lowered by conducting several elections the same day. And voter apathy ought to be decreased through better education, although that is certainly easier said than done. An advantage of multiple parliaments would be that voters could tailor their vote to the issue at hand, for instance by voting for a left-wing party for an intergovernmental organization in charge of civil and political rights promotion, and for a right-wing party for another organization in charge of economic policies. On the other hand, a disadvantage of multiple parliaments would be the impossibility of making deals across policy areas.

On the European continent, several intergovernmental organizations have had parliaments, including the European Union, the Council of Europe (a human rights organization), and the Western European Union (a defense organization). Some of these parliaments are not directly elected but rather consist of delegates of national parliaments, which is another option other intergovernmental organizations might emulate. Some of these parliaments are purely consultative, but others have real decision-making powers. Creating consultative parliaments consisting of delegates of national parliaments, then progressively increasing their decision-making power and the proportion of directly elected parliamentarians, is a way to incrementally shift control of intergovernmental organizations away from national executive branches to global parliaments, which is more in line with global democracy for the reasons laid out in the previous paragraphs.

Such an incremental process is explicitly envisaged in the protocol establishing the African Union parliament, for instance. That said, representatives of national governments could very well continue to play a major role in most or all intergovernmental organizations, with shared decision making between them and the organizations' directly elected parliaments. Such power sharing between two legislative bodies exists in most federations (e.g., the Senate and House of Representatives in the United States). Again, only one legislative body, either representing national governments or directly elected, is strictly necessary for global democracy, and the existence of both is usually a compromise solution reflecting the importance of multiple political communities: that of the federation and those of the federated entities.

Parliaments of intergovernmental organizations could be very large. For example, with one representative for every million inhabitants, a universal intergovernmental organization would have a parliament of more than six thousand representatives. However, this size ought not represent a problem thanks to communication technologies and adequate protocols. All parliamentarians would not even need to meet physically, for instance. But information technologies do not mark the end of representative democracy in favor of direct democracy. There will always be a need for professional politicians who can process the information that computers freely transmit, and to make deals.

THE PREVIOUS PARAGRAPHS NOTWITHSTANDING, civil and political rights would continue to be matters decided mainly at the national level of government. Yet global democracy would necessitate some minimum global standards because it would not be possible to develop a democracy at the global level of government in the absence of democracy at the national level. It is hard to imagine dictatorships allowing their citizens to freely express opinions about global public policy issues, and possibly to run for elections of intergovernmental organizations' parliaments, if the dictatorships fail to uphold such rights for national policy making. While some dictatorships represent their people's interests in international forums fairly decently, others do not, and even the former are generally more likely to be manipulated by special interests than democratic governments. That is why human rights entry tests for second-tier intergovernmental organizations ought to be an essential institutional feature of global democracy.

The European Union is the intergovernmental organization that has applied human rights entry tests at their fullest. Candidates for membership must incorporate far-reaching civil and political rights in their national legislations, and have functioning and independent judiciaries to enforce them. Moreover, all European Union members are also members of the Council of Europe, and their citizens can therefore sue their governments at the European Court of Human Rights if national courts did not handle their case well. Human rights tests exist on other continents as well. For example, the Organization of American States bars participation of unelected governments, such as Cuba at present.

Agreeing on a human rights entry test is a delicate matter, as different countries have different understandings of what constitute human rights. This old human rights debate pits universalists, who insist on the universality of core rights regardless of national contexts, and relativists, who prefer to adapt rights to cultural circumstances even at the danger of weakening them. In fact, people disagree on what ought to constitute human rights even within any given country. That is not surprising because, when it comes to detailed interpretations of broad rights (e.g., the right to security, the right to privacy), one right often clashes with another (e.g., limiting privacy to fight terrorism). In the United States, for instance, rights issues that remain heavily contested include gay marriage, abortion, the death penalty, affirmative action, school prayer, stem-cell research, the tension between free speech and political campaign finance laws, and more. It is hard enough for any American politician to arbitrate such internal debates without foreign interference, and it would therefore be quite understandable that such politicians would resent having to agree with Europeans on North Atlantic standards, given that Europeans tend to be more libertarian on some issues (e.g., the death penalty) and less on others (e.g., campaign finance).

Such differences on a range of specific civil rights ought not be a problem, however. For the primary goal of human rights entry tests is to ensure that citizens can participate in global political processes. Hence, human rights entry tests should generally be strong enough to exclude states where political debate is significantly repressed, but otherwise be sufficiently lenient as to allow all other states to join. A human rights entry test slightly more demanding than that of the Organization of

American States would probably be adequate for most second-tier intergovernmental organizations.

Many states would find themselves on the borderline of the Organization of American States' human rights entry test. For instance, they may have elected governments but elections might not really be contested for a range of reasons, such as a civil war in part of the country or a tightly controlled press. It is for these cases that human rights entry tests need to be precise. It is also for these cases that the tests can play an important secondary role: promoting alignment toward higher civil and political rights standards. States falling not too far short of a human rights entry test would face a powerful incentive to advance their citizens' civil and political rights to meet that test, the more so if the benefits they would derive from membership of any given intergovernmental organization were high. The experience of applicants to the European Union (e.g., Turkey today, Southern and Eastern European states in the past) has demonstrated the power of that incentive. Based on that experience, one could argue to raise the bar of human rights entry tests significantly beyond that of the Organization of American States and closer to that of the European Union. But that could defeat the purpose of inclusiveness of global democracy. Yet that might be appropriate for some organizations, such as the reformed and expanded NATO described in Chapter 13, on the ground that would-be NATO members ought to provide strong guarantees of internal stability to their allies and that civil peace heavily depends on strong civil and political rights.

Human rights entry tests would not represent an incentive for dictatorial regimes to improve their civil and political rights records. Such states would rather secede or not join second-tier intergovernmental organizations, and thus forfeit the benefits attached to them such as defense guarantees, foreign aid, or more favorable trade relations. Isolation from such organizations might modestly weaken dictatorships. For example, the current isolation of the regimes of Syria and Myanmar by the international community does make them somewhat more vulnerable to internal coups or popular uprisings, especially in a long-term perspective. It is one thing to be isolated and backward for now, another to have been so for the past half century. But that is by no means a powerful instrument to advance civil and political rights in such countries in the short term. Short of outright invasion, which should be reserved for the most outrageous human rights violations of genocide or crimes against humanity, there simply are no good international instruments to prompt reform of dictatorial regimes. Global democracy would therefore not add much to the panoply of weak instruments currently used by the United Nations to promote human rights in dictatorships, beyond the fact that the existence of second-tier organizations would increase the isolation of such regimes. It is for countries at the borderline of decency that global democracy would be most useful as far as the advancement of civil and political rights is concerned, thanks to the human rights entry test.

IN SUMMARY, GLOBAL DEMOCRACY could create, though would not absolutely necessitate, new political and civil rights at the global level of government, notably the rights for citizens to sue intergovernmental organizations and to elect and stand for election in global parliaments. On the other hand, global democracy absolutely requires minimum civil and political rights at the national level of government, without which people could not fully participate in global political debates. Human rights entry tests for second-tier intergovernmental organizations are a powerful way to meet such minimum standards for all but the most authoritarian states, which would presumably not participate in global democracy.

15

Promotion of Economic and Social Rights

$\mathcal{S}$IGNS OF EMERGING GLOBAL democracy are most visible in the global economic policy area. The World Trade Organization (WTO), set up in 1994, is one of the most powerful and innovative global intergovernmental organizations ever created. A dense network of transnational civil society organizations has risen as a counterpower to that organization. Once marginalized poor and middle-income countries have started to assert their right to participate in decision making. The WTO is now at a crossroads and will eventually have to choose between democratization and marginalization.

What is the global democratic approach to global trade policy?

The global democratic approach to international trade is that its regulation should be decided by the majority of the world population or, at the least, the majority of the combined populations of states that choose to become members of intergovernmental organizations competent for trade regulation. Global democracy is therefore agnostic about the globalization debate. If a majority of the world population favored greater economic globalization, then restrictions on the movement of goods and services should be reduced. If not, they should be strengthened.

Both positions have merits, and in my opinion the right policy course is a pragmatic approach to each specific trade issue, balancing the interests of all concerned parties in a democratic way.[12] On the one hand, globalization is good for economic development because global markets allow for deeper division of labor through economies of scale, and division of labor is a primary driver of wealth creation. For instance, the city where I live, Cambridge, Massachusetts, has a gross domestic product larger than that of Senegal and about forty-five other countries. One would not expect Cambridge folks to produce everything to meet their own consumption needs: cars, computers, clothes, insurance services, and so on. It is obviously more productive for them to concentrate their work on what they do best (i.e., higher education), and import what they need from other towns. So one should not expect countries that are smaller than Cambridge in economic terms to be as self-sufficient as possible—however you define "possible."

Similarly, the gross domestic product of the Netherlands is larger that that of the whole African continent. Yet the Netherlands is a small economy by North American and European standards. To compensate for its small size, the Netherlands heavily relies on international trade to take advantage of the efficiency that division of labor entails. This suggests that even a pan-African free-trade area would need to rely heavily on imports from and exports to the rest of the world to achieve successful economic development.

On the other hand, proponents of free trade too often make the big leap between the correct premise that international trade is generally good for economic development and the incorrect conclusion that all national governments should adopt across-the-board free-trade policies. First, history shows that almost no country has ever developed on a free-trade policy. Most countries, like China and India today, Japan and South Korea in recent decades, and Britain and the United States in past centuries, relied on international trade but heavily regulated it to their advantage.[13]

Second, the short- and medium-term social costs of long-term economic development should not be dismissed lightly. Like technological progress, trade creates wealth by rendering some economic activities obsolete in certain locations, thereby wreaking havoc in communities and particularly in poor people's lives. Depending on local circumstances, some people may never recover from the loss of their livelihoods, or they may recover only after extreme hardship. For small farmers who live literally at the edge of subsistence, a reduction in import tariffs on their crops, which would increase foreign competition, can be the difference between life and death.

Third, trade regulations are never politically or morally neutral. "Free trade"—or the absence of restrictions on cross-border economic activity—is an ideal that is not practical for the real world. Even free traders call for a minimum of international rules and enforcement mechanisms to foster international trade. Details of such regulations have important implications for the distribution of income and wealth among interest groups within and across borders. The free-trade ideology is too often invoked by interest groups to pursue their own lowly interests.

The democratic political process is thus the fairest way to arbitrate the different views on the role of trade in development, the trade-offs between long-term development and the short- and medium-term social costs it entails, and the conflicts among special interests that any regulation generates.

To EXPLORE HOW TO move in the direction of global democracy on trade issues, it is worth examining the institutional features of the WTO, which is currently the most important intergovernmental organization regulating the movement of goods and services at the global level. The WTO has many of the institutional features of global democracy. It is a second-tier organization that does not have universal membership, as the United Nations does, because it requires strong discipline from its member-states to follow the rules it sets (feature 1). Yet it is potentially open to all states in the world who accept those rules (feature 6: free entry), and is actually steadily increasing its membership. Member-states have the right to secede from it (feature 2). And the WTO even has a sort of independent judicial authority in the form of the Dispute Settlement Body (feature 8).

Most importantly, the WTO is a federal organization, since it restricts both opt-out and veto rights (features 3 and 4). Opt-out rights are limited in that all member-states must abide by all provisions of all sixty "multilateral trade agreements" that have been developed in the framework of the WTO or its predecessor, the General Agreement on

Tariffs and Trade. (Trade agreements have a status roughly equivalent to treaties.) This lack of opt-out rights marks a sharp difference between the trade policy area and the civil and political rights or environmental policy areas, where states may freely choose to opt in or out of treaties negotiated at the United Nations, or even adopt them with specific reservations. Together, the multilateral trade agreements form a considerable corpus of global economic policies—about thirty thousand pages of legal text—covering economic transactions in many aspects, from sanitary regulations for agricultural products to the prohibition of export subsidies for manufacturing goods.

The WTO nevertheless gives its member-states a great deal of flexibility to apply its rules, through what I will call "authorized opt-out rights." Authorized opt-out rights are opt-out rights that member-states may not exercise unilaterally, but only with the agreement of other member-states and generally under tight conditions. They come in a variety of forms. First, the WTO statutes stipulate that a three-fourths majority of member-states can exempt any member-state from endorsing any specific provisions of any trade agreement. However, such waivers must be temporary and justified by exceptional circumstances, and they may be subject to conditions.

Second, many trade agreements attach different obligations to different classes of member-states: "least developed economies" (i.e., poorest countries), "developing economies" (i.e., poor and middle-income countries), and "transition economies" (i.e., formerly communist countries). These so-called "special and differential treatments" usually exempt the poorest countries from some rules, and give longer transition periods for the two other classes to implement them. That is the case, for example, for rules on intellectual property (i.e., patents, copyrights, trademarks).

Third, some trade agreements allow member-states to temporarily waive their compliance with some rules if they can demonstrate that certain circumstances prevail and if they comply with certain monitoring provisions. That is the case of so-called safeguard clauses that allow member-states to impose temporary import tariffs to protect an industry from a sudden surge of imports. These clauses are regularly used and often abused, but there is a mechanism to discipline member-states back into compliance.

Fourth, and most importantly, the multilateral trade agreements themselves add up to little over five hundred pages. The thirty thousand pages of legal texts I referred to earlier consist mostly of country-specific appendices, called "schedules of concessions and commitments." The trade agreements lay out general rules, but the schedules contain very specific obligations for each member-state. In that way, the maximum import tariffs that member-states are allowed to levy on a given manufactured good, say, televisions, can vary across member-states but must be approved by all member-states. That is the archetype of an authorized opt-out right, which allows for both flexibility and discipline: member-states may tailor some obligations to their national interests but may not unilaterally invent exemptions for themselves.

Finally, four of the sixty trade agreements of the WTO are known as "plurilateral" instead of "multilateral" trade agreements, which means that member-states may opt out of them. One of them is the agreement on government procurement, for instance. Plurilateral agreements represent a regular opt-out right, an exception to the general ban on opt-out rights at the WTO.

As to veto rights, the decision-making practice at the WTO has been that of consensus, which suggests that every member-state has a veto right. However, the statutes of the organization stipulate that, if consensus cannot be found, most decisions can be taken by simple or qualified majority voting, each member-state having one vote. In particular, amendments to trade agreements require a two-thirds majority of member-states, and a three-fourths majority may decide to expel from the WTO those member-states that refuse to endorse the approved amendments. Adoption of entirely new trade agreements is one of the few kinds of decisions requiring strict consensus, and member-states have the right to opt out of such new agreements. However, the reach of this rule is limited since existing trade agreements already cover most trade-related issues.

These statutory decision-making rules are not used because diplomats prefer to project an image of consensus. But they underpin negotiations because national government officials know that, if push came to shove and a vote were called, they could be outvoted and eventually face the embarrassing situation of presenting their national parliaments with legislation that they have officially opposed in order to avoid expulsion from the WTO.

Only a handful of member-states can actually exercise their veto right, and each member-state's actual influence over WTO decisions is directly proportional to its weight in global trade. The United States, the European Union, and Japan have the capacity to veto any amendments at the WTO, thereby imposing the status quo on all member-states. They accept rules they do not like only to the extent that they obtain reciprocal concessions from their trade partners. That veto capacity stems from their credible secession threat: If a package of new trade rules that they did not approve of overall were to pass, they would secede, and the WTO would collapse. We have one global economy and it would be inconceivable for, say, Japanese multinational companies to play by other rules than American and European companies.

By contrast, Bangladesh has a population equal to that of Japan but the value of its international trade is fifty times lower. The Bangladeshi trade minister knows intimately that it would be inconceivable for him or her to veto new trade rules that the United States, the European Union, and Japan all want. If he or she were to formally object to a new rule, a vote could ensue, which Bangladesh would presumably lose, and the big trading powers could even call for a vote to expel Bangladesh from the WTO. The secession, voluntary or forced, of a country like Bangladesh would not produce much stress on the global economy. Many countries are not yet part of the WTO anyway, even countries as big as Russia. China joined only in 2001. At the time, multinational companies from the United States, the European Union, and Japan did find China's isolation from the system of global trade rules bothersome—although they could still live with it—and that is why there was support for China to become a member. The China episode provides an idea of the size one country needs to be to have a voice at the WTO.

No one WTO member save the United States, the European Union, and Japan is truly indispensable to the global economy. Other major trading powers such as Australia, Brazil, Canada, China, India, Mexico, South Korea, Switzerland, or Taiwan do have real influence, especially on issues relevant to industries for which they are particularly strong. (I dwell on their growing influence later on.) But they are vulnerable to being arm-twisted into agreement by a coalition of the big three and other countries. Smaller countries have either negligible or no influence on trade rules at all, except on their own schedule of concessions and commitments—though they are vulnerable to arm-twisting about these rules as well. That lack of influence is reflected in that they are oftentimes not even invited to the table of informal negotiations where big compromises are hashed out.

In other words, from the perspective of the United States, the European Union, and Japan, every one of the WTO's thirty thousand pages of legal texts is up for negotiation. When deals for new rules are reached, they face the choice between accepting them or imposing the status quo on all member-states by exercising their veto right. By contrast, from the perspective of poor countries, the WTO is thirty-thousand-pages worth of legal texts to be accepted almost on a take-it-or-leave-it basis. Every time the big three trading powers reach a new agreement among themselves, other countries face a quite different choice: either accepting it or seceding from the WTO—the status quo ceases to be an option for them. By depriving most of its member-states of the effective ability of either vetoing or opting out of its trade agreements, the WTO has achieved world federalism by stealth.

How would global democracy help promote fair global trade?

Joining or staying in the WTO or not is thus one of the biggest and most difficult decisions that national parliaments must make. On the one hand, the lack of opt-out rights does curtail national governments' policy options to foster national economic development.[14] On the other hand, staying out of the WTO means isolating oneself from the global economy, which can have very negative consequences for national economic development as well.

The main advantage of WTO membership is the protection of the so-called most-favored-nation clause, which means that all member-states are entitled to the best trading conditions offered by each member-state. In other words, the WTO does not allow favoritism or discrimination among its member-states. Historically, the United States and the European Union have made a lot of concessions toward each other in terms of lowering trade barriers. Thanks to the most-favored-nation clause, other member-states have benefited from these lower barriers as well. (The flip side of that history is that the trading giants have delayed the liberalization of some industries where both of them were very vulnerable to competition from poor countries, particularly agriculture and the textile industry.) States that choose not to join the WTO or to secede from it must negotiate bilateral trade agreements with each of their trading partners, and nothing mitigates economic power imbalances in such negotiations: Secessionists cannot count on the support of member-states that have similar trade interests but more influence.

This reality is also why weak confederalism is not the solution for obtaining fair trade rules. If the WTO were to close down and global trade policy were taken over by the United Nations, rich countries could opt out of any trade rules they did not like. To the extent that poor and middle-income countries did want to promote trade relations with rich ones, they would need to rely on regional or bilateral trade agreements in which they could not count on the extension of concessions made by rich countries to each other. The outcome of bilateral and regional negotiations would therefore be even less fair. Weak confederalism only makes sense if a goal of national economic policy is to minimize trade relations, a goal consistent with localism.

Despite the loss of control over national economic policy that it entails, most countries have chosen to join the WTO, or are taking steps toward accession. Free traders argue that that choice legitimizes the WTO. The WTO's legitimacy actually depends upon one's moral reference point. If one's reference point is the law of the jungle or anarchy, where bilateral balance of power determines the rules of trading relations, then the WTO indeed offers some protections to poor countries. But if one's reference point is democratic decision making, then the WTO is illegitimate. The WTO is an apartheid organization: It institutionalizes inequality between poor and rich countries. Poor countries may well decide that institutional inequality is better than raw inequality or anarchy. But that does not make institutional inequality legitimate.

The institutionalized inequality among WTO member-states has a direct impact on the quality of the trade rules it promulgates. The campaigning group Oxfam has highlighted a series of rigged rules and double standards in the global trade policy area.[15] The manipulation of global trade rules to maximize the profits of special interests is not an unfortunate side effect of the pursuit of trade liberalization: It is the name of the game at the WTO. And because poor people have negligible influence, they are too often the victims of that game.[16]

Under pressure from poor and middle-income countries and campaigning groups like Oxfam, rich countries have implicitly acknowledged that the system was wrong when they agreed that the current round of WTO negotiations be called the "Doha Development Round" and should "seek to place [poor and middle-income countries'] needs and interests at the heart of the [negotiations]."[17] Asking some WTO member-states to take to heart the interests of other member-states over their own does not, of course, make any more sense than asking parliamentarians to listen to the electorate of the constituency next to theirs instead of their own or asking shareholders to endorse business plans that maximize the profits of their competitors instead of their own. It is therefore not at all surprising that rich countries have failed to deliver on their promise.[18] Shaming rich countries into behaving more morally than the institutions induce them to behave is a first step toward democratizing global trade policy making. But it has clear limits. Sooner rather than later, poor and middle-income countries as well as trade justice campaigning groups ought to demand the democratization of the institutions themselves.

THERE ARE ONLY A couple of institutional features of global democracy that the WTO does not have: majority voting with equal universal suffrage (one person, one vote), and the human rights entry test (features 7 and 5, respectively). Adopting the former would require just a couple of amendments to the WTO statutes: weighing votes according to population, and lowering majority thresholds to simple majority for amendments to existing trade agreements and to, say, a majority of two thirds for the adoption of new agreements.

The "one state, one vote" decision-making rule that prevails at the WTO, and in many other intergovernmental organizations, just does not make sense. It is ridiculous that representatives of St. Kitts and Nevis, population 41,000, have as much voting power as representatives of China, population 1,250,000,000. Such nonsense is actually an additional reason why voting does not usually take place at the WTO or in most other intergovernmental organizations. The "one state, one vote" rule is practiced at the United Nations General Assembly and other weak confederations mostly to make nonbinding decisions. In that sense, voting is little more than opinion polling. Although it is also used at the Security Council where decisions matter a great deal, it is mostly irrelevant because of the vetoes that the five permanent members can wield.

The shift to equal universal suffrage at the WTO would of course amount to a revolution. However, as illustrated by the history of universal suffrage in Britain in the introduction to this book, it could take place incrementally over several decades, as the idea of global democracy gains overwhelming momentum. One incremental option would be to renegotiate the voting distribution periodically, starting from a distribution that overrepresents little populated member-states and underrepresents populous ones (as has been done at the European Union). Transitional voting distributions could also, as a temporary concession to realpolitik, overrepresent member-states with large shares of global trade flows. Another temporary solution could be to adopt decisions with the positive vote or abstention of a handful of member-states that are either big trading powers or very populous (e.g., the United States, the European Union, Japan, China, and India), plus a majority of middle-sized trading powers (e.g., Australia, Brazil, Canada, Mexico, South Korea), plus a simple majority of all other member-states, with votes weighted according to population. Such a rule would improve though not dramatically change the current balance of power, would introduce the notion of majority voting, and would expose the veto rights of the few big member-states as an oddity and privilege to be abolished in time.

In parallel with the couple of statute amendments necessary to introduce majority voting with equal universal suffrage, democratizing the WTO would also require a change in practice, moving from consensual decision making to regular majority voting. As shown in previous paragraphs, consensus decision making has been deceptive, and equal universal suffrage would become meaningful only if votes were actually taken. Consensus also makes decision making quite unwieldy, forcing negotiators to package ever more complex issues in order to find deals that are, overall, acceptable to all major players. In particular, consensus can lead to paralysis when the number of veto-wielding actors multiplies. Regular majority voting on discrete policy decisions would facilitate decision making. Negotiations at the WTO and its predecessor, the General Agreement on Tariffs and Trade, have hitherto been difficult, marathon exercises concluding every decade or two with mammoth package deals covering a range of issues such that each veto-wielding state can find enough benefits to justify its own concessions. As the number of players "too big to ignore" increases, deals are likely to become increasingly hard to reach under such a negotiation setup. By contrast, regular voting on discrete issues would expedite decision making. The price to pay would be that some member-states would lose votes and be bound to accept rules they do not like. Nevertheless, states might lose a vote one day and win another the next day, and generally remain satisfied with membership in the WTO—or be free to leave.

Voting would also make decision making more transparent and increase the ability of citizens to hold their policy makers accountable. For even in the context of the current marathon rounds of trade negotiations, discrete decisions on individual, narrow issues are being made. But they are made during informal and closed-door negotiating sessions among the representatives of a handful of big trading powers.

When the shift to majority voting with equal universal suffrage were eventually introduced, Americans and Europeans would start experiencing the WTO in the same way as poor and middle-income countries have: as a federal organization. To fulfill the aspiration of global democracy, big powers would need to accept majority decisions that they themselves do not endorse, just as France and Germany do when they are outvoted in the European Union's Council.

Majority rule with equal universal suffrage would undoubtedly shift the balance of power and lead to a long-term reversal of current rigged trade rules, again in the same way as universal suffrage in Britain enabled a shift from unbridled capitalism to a mixed social market economy.

On the other hand, the danger that equal universal suffrage would lead poor countries to take advantage of their voting power and impose sudden and highly redistributive trade rules that would wreak havoc in rich countries' economies would be low for several reasons. First, poor countries would not have an interest in damaging the economies of rich ones, because it would destabilize the whole global economy and harm all countries.

Second, the coming decades are likely to see a growth of the global middle class, with continued brisk growth in East and Southeast Asia, for instance. The danger would actually be that the global upper and middle classes (regardless of national origin) would drive policies that would further marginalize the poorest minority. Such phenomena can sometimes be observed at the national level of government, where politicians pander to the middle class while neglecting the really poor.

That consideration leads to a third point: Poor people are usually less well-organized politically, and elites often manage to hold onto power, at least for some time, thanks to their privileged education, access to information and networks, and of course money, which plays a significant role in the electoral processes of most countries. Previous democratic power sharing by a rich minority with a poor majority, such as the adoption of equal universal suffrage in Britain or the end of apartheid in South Africa in 1994, have been fairly smooth for these reasons as well.

A last reason a global democratic WTO is unlikely to produce sudden, highly redistributive policies is that member-states would keep their secession right. Rich countries could continue to use the threat of secession, implicitly or explicitly, as leverage in trade negotiations. They could leave the WTO and recreate among themselves an intergovernmental organization to set new international trade rules. Once established by the richest countries, such an organization would gradually attract some poor and middle-income countries accepting rigged rules and double standards in order to acquire limited access to rich countries' markets. Because the geographical scope of such an organization would be reduced to a subset of the global economy, it would not be an optimal solution for rich countries. But it would remain a fallback position in the face of over-the-top redistributive rules pushed by a global democratic WTO. That is why global democracy is not merely an institutional reform agenda, but also an attitude toward global public policy; global democrats should resist such temptation of secession. But there is no doubt that officials of rich member-states would use that leverage in the early days of a global democratic WTO. Nevertheless, as the practice of majority voting with equal universal suffrage gradually becomes entrenched in everyone's conception of world politics, that leverage will become increasingly difficult to wield, both morally and politically.

Besides majority voting with equal universal suffrage, the other feature of global democracy that the WTO does not yet have is the human rights entry test. Despite the absence of such an entry test, the most brutal dictators have kept their countries outside of the WTO. This situation is probably not a coincidence since there is some relationship between economic liberalism and the respect of civil rights, if not political rights. The general free entry rule of the WTO (feature 6 of global democracy) has also been compromised as the United States and the European Union have been using admission to the WTO as a tool of foreign policy to keep some countries out (e.g., Iran) or extort from them political concessions unrelated to trade policy (e.g., guarantees for nuclear disarmament). Such an ad hoc approach to human rights is no substitute for objective human rights guarantees because it unavoidably leads to double standards (why China and not Iran?) and feeds enmity of those left out.

There are, however, a number of WTO member-states that are governed by officials who have not come to power through contested elections. China is of course the most significant example. Unelected governments do not necessarily fail to represent their people decently as far as global trade policy is concerned. Again, China is an example of an authoritarian regime that does fairly well in defending its nationals' economic interests. But there clearly are examples of WTO member-states whose governments really ought not be entrusted with the power to cast votes proportional to the size of the population that they fail to actually represent. In a global democratic perspective, these member-states ought to be expelled from the WTO, although they could remain integrated into the global trade rules system through separate treaties that would grant them all WTO privileges except for decision-making rights.

Human rights entry tests can vary from one intergovernmental organization to the other. I argued for a fairly tight entry test in the global security policy area, ensuring not only real political representation but also effective enforcement of civil rights such as to decrease the likelihood of civil war. A more relaxed entry test may be warranted in the global trade policy area. An argument was made during debates around Chinese accession to the WTO that bringing authoritarian regimes into the fold of a liberal global trade regime would, over the long term, foster an entrepreneurial middle class that would demand political rights. Such argument has merits, but it should be balanced with the need for proper representation.

Part of the human rights entry test at the WTO could be effective enforcement of specific labor rights, such as the core rights of nondiscrimination of employees, prohibition of child labor, freedom of association of employees, and collective bargaining. Labor rights are not only human rights but also economic regulations that arguably fall into the WTO's logical competences, even though they are not WTO competences yet. WTO rules restrict the maneuvering room of national governments in order to protect the interests of consumers as well as shareholders throughout the world. But they do not protect the third big economic interest group: workers. Yet even though workers' migration remains restricted, they are part of the global economy: There is a global labor market. Corporations are free to shop around the world for the cheapest labor. Workers should be free to organize transnationally in order to gain bargaining power vis-à-vis transnational corporations. That is obviously possible only if they are able to organize nationally in the first place, which calls for minimum international labor standards. There is also an argument to be made for consumers' right to guarantees that the products they purchase have not been produced through processes that violate human rights.[19]

Making labor rights a competence of the WTO has not been a priority of the powerful economic interests that drive the WTO (i.e., capital owners) for obvious reasons. But that move has also been opposed by governments of poor and middle-income countries, for fear that labor unions in rich countries would manipulate the rules to protect their workers at the expense of workers in poor countries. Given the institutionalized inequality at the WTO, such fear is well warranted. But the democratization of the WTO should allay them. Thanks to their voting power, poor and middle-income countries would be able to reject labor standards that do not suit their interests.

In the end, making labor rights a WTO competence is a political decision, which according to global democracy should be made by a qualified majority of member-states with votes weighted by population. Once the WTO adopted an "agreement on trade-related labor rights," any amendments to it could then be passed by simple majority. Meanwhile, labor rights should of course continue to be advanced through the International Labor Organization according to weak confederalism, that is, on a purely voluntary basis. In the global democratic framework, the International Labor Organization would remain a first-tier intergovernmental organization.

THERE IS ONE ADDITIONAL institutional reform that would be desirable, although not absolutely necessary, to democratize the WTO: creating a parliamentary assembly. A parliamentary assembly could, for example, be elected directly by nationals of all WTO member-states according to their respective electoral laws and each member-state could have one seat for every million nationals. The parliamentary assembly could be a consultative body at its inception, and eventually gain the same decision-making rights as the Ministerial Conference.

Global parliaments are not necessary to global democracy because what matters in the end is the respect of the "one person, one vote" rule, and national government representatives in intergovernmental organizations do represent their populations (at least if they pass a sufficient human rights entry test). But states are odd constituencies to aggregate preferences about global trade policy. Some are very large; others are so small that their weighted votes would rightfully be negligible. Some states (the smaller ones) would have fairly homogenous constituents; others would have very diverse constituencies.

Even though national governments accountable to national constituencies and national interest groups remain the sole decision makers at the WTO for the time being, transnational interest groups such as multinational companies, international trade associations, international associations of labor unions or consumers, and various campaigning groups are already asserting influence over global trade policy. That influence would increase if decision-making power at the WTO were shared between representatives of national governments and directly elected parliamentarians. Since parliamentarians would be accountable to subnational and therefore even smaller constituencies than representatives of national governments, they would likely defend narrower economic interests.

For example, parliamentarians from rural districts could defend rural interests only, while national representatives would need to balance both rural and urban interests. Rural parliamentarians would naturally build coalitions with their peers in other countries, and these transnational coalitions would be receptive to pressure from transnational interest groups defending rural interests.

I mentioned above that the WTO sets mostly broad rules, and grants extensive authorized opt-out rights for precise rules to vary across its member-states, particularly through the schedules of concessions and commitments. The creation of a parliamentary assembly at the WTO would probably lead it to make more precise transnational rules, thereby curtailing authorized opt-out rights.

The creation of a parliamentary assembly—or at least its assumption of binding decision-making power—would probably be resisted by the national government officials who currently monopolize power at the WTO because it would be a loss of power for them. It may therefore happen even later than the adoption of majority voting with equal universal suffrage. But transnational economic interests do become more powerful as the global economy increasingly integrates, and as global civil society grows through increased transnational exchange of information. The pressure to regulate the global economy through transnational rules applying everywhere, such as the current minimum intellectual property rights, rather than through guidelines from which member-states can agree to deviate, such as tariff rates on individual commodities, is already a reality.

Is that trend toward more transnational rules a good thing for what should be the ultimate objective of global trade policy: promoting global economic development for all and particularly the poorest? To close this argument on the effect of global democracy on global trade policy, it is useful to recast the global trade debate in a new light. As Oxfam's report *Rigged Rules and Double Standards* asserts, the debate is not about more or less globalization, but about fair rules.[20] In this book, I have argued that federalism with equal universal suffrage is necessary to obtain fair rules. That said, once poor and middle-income countries were empowered at the WTO, that organization could fight global poverty in two quite different ways that would imply different depths of economic globalization.

One direction for global trade policy could be to renationalize economic policy by increasing the reliance on authorized opt-out rights. Poor and middle-income countries would be allowed to pursue national economic policies by heavily regulating their international trade in idiosyncratic ways, in the same ways as rich countries have done to industrialize in past centuries. For example, the WTO could set new trade-related rules on investment and services, but the majority of the world population could demand that poor and middle-income countries receive extensive exemptions from them. That path has been advocated by a number of progressive economists, such as Dani Rodrik of Harvard University and Ha-Joon Chang of the University of Cambridge.[21]

Alternatively, a global democratic WTO could deepen globalization by producing fairer transnational rules, rules that apply uniformly everywhere with fewer authorized opt-out rights. A progressive agenda could include less aggressive liberalization of trade in goods and services with fairer rules on intellectual property and investment, and new global rules on labor rights and competition policy. In other words, the world population could demand rules that would deepen global economic integration and significantly reduce the maneuvering room of national governments to manage their economies, provided that they fairly rebalance the interests of workers with those of shareholders and consumers, and of poor people with those of rich people.

Rodrik makes a nice analysis of these two directions for global economic policy, and advocates for renationalization in the short to medium term, while leaving the door open for deeper but fairer globalization in the long term.[22] Both paths are compatible with federalism and global democracy, although the emergence of a global community does create a bias toward the latter in the long term. They are feasible within the same federal institutional framework, which implies that the transition from one to the other could be smooth. Indeed, both paths could be partially implemented at the same time. For example, the WTO could set tight minimum labor standards for its member-states while allowing for more extensive authorized opt-out rights on intellectual property or import tariffs than it does today.

It is useful for advocates of progressive economic policies to realize that the debate is not about federalism or confederalism, but rather between authorized opt-out rights and the lack of them. Federalism is necessary to achieve trade justice because nothing mitigates imbalances of power among states in weak confederations. But federalism can be made flexible and leave room for national policy making thanks to authorized opt-out rights.

A final comment on the fight against poverty and authorized opt-out rights concerns the issue that could be called "affirmative action" in global trade policy. The WTO currently has a sort of affirmative action policy: the special and differential treatments that allow middle-income and poor countries to either delay implementation or opt out of certain rules. There are arguments on both sides of the debate over affirmative action in general—whether it indeed promotes unprivileged minorities or whether it only promotes the minority's most privileged at the expense of the majority's least privileged.

Affirmative action poses a special problem in democracies when the "minority" it seeks to promote actually constitutes the majority of the population, which would be the case for poor countries in a democratic WTO. (It is also the case in South Africa, where the Black Economic Empowerment policy, which promotes control of enterprises by black people, has become a national joke.) It would not be healthy for the majority to set rules it could itself opt out of. It would be preferable for the WTO statutes to limit any special and differential treatments to the so-called least developed countries, which do represent a minority in terms of population.

Affirmative action could also be introduced in the form of transnational rules applying to all member-states. For example, the WTO statutes could define several categories of companies (e.g., domestic or multinational; or small, middle-sized, and big companies depending on the number of employees) and adjust various trade agreements to exempt small companies from certain rules, regardless of their national origin or location. That would allow, for instance, setting high labor standards for all multinational companies as well as large domestic companies throughout the world, less stringent standards for small companies, and of course no global standard for the informal sector, which by definition falls outside the law. Most countries used such differentiated approach to introduce labor rights at the national level, and poor countries might be more willing to accept labor rights mandated by the WTO along that approach as well.

What political forces could bring about global democracy?

A lot of progress toward global democracy has already been achieved in the area of economic policy. Indeed, I have noted that the WTO is a couple of statutory amendments away from it. The essential missing piece is equal universal suffrage. Moreover, the three political forces I mentioned in the introduction—global civil society, rising middle-income powers, and enlightened elites—are already struggling over the "democratic deficit" of the organization.

The rise in influence of populous poor and middle-income countries like Brazil, China, and India at the WTO is one of the two tectonic shifts that have occurred in world politics over the past five years (the other being the emerging clash of civilizations between Islam and the West following the attacks of September 11, 2001). When I conceived this book a few years ago, I anticipated that fast-paced economic growth in Asia was bound to bring about some democratization of the WTO, merely on the grounds that influence at the WTO is directly proportional to a country's share of world trade. I did not anticipate that it would occur so quickly—indeed, it has been faster than my writing about it!

At that time, most articles on the WTO included references to the "Quad." The Quad is an informal group of four big trading partners: the United States, the European Union, Japan, and Canada. It used to meet in so-called green rooms to thrash out big decisions before presenting them to the whole WTO membership as near faits accomplis. (The Quad typically invited middle-sized trading partners to their informal deliberations to deal with specific topics, but it controlled the agenda and invitation list.)

Although the green-room process still exists, it has become more transparent and its membership has changed. I read fewer references to the Quad these days, but I have discovered the new acronym BRIC, standing for Brazil, Russia, India, and China.[23] (Russia is not yet a WTO member but nevertheless a rising power in global economic policy.) In the past, negotiations failed only when the United States and the European Union could not agree with each other. But when WTO Director-General Pascal Lamy made the heavy decision to indefinitely suspend the Doha Development Round of trade negotiations on July 24, 2006, he did so after an informal meeting of trade ministers of Australia, Brazil, the European Union, India, Japan, and the United States. Canada was out, but Brazil and India were in and the pressure they exerted on the European Union and the United States contributed to the outcome. (Australia was invited to represent the free-trade camp on agricultural policy, as the meeting focused mostly on that sector.) I would characterize that change in the composition of the green room as a significant incremental step toward equal universal suffrage.

Nevertheless, the next steps remain tantalizingly ambitious and are likely to require several decades of advocacy—and the whole project could yet flounder. The first problem with the emancipation of the BRIC, or more generally of the "global middle class" of "emerging economies" like Mexico, Singapore, South Korea, South Africa, Taiwan, and, a little further behind, Malaysia, Thailand, and others, is that it leaves behind the "global lower class," mainly most of the African continent.

Before its suspension, the Doha Development Round generated a special negotiation process to resolve a dispute over the subsidies that some WTO members, mainly the United States, pay to their cotton farmers. Those subsidies create unfair competition with cotton farmers in the rest of the world, including those in very poor African countries. The process was set up at the initiative of four African states for which cotton is a vital industry—Benin, Chad, Mali, and Togo—and with the support of campaigning groups like Oxfam. Rarely had African governments been that assertive at the WTO in the past. Yet, had Brazil and India agreed to a deal with the European Union, the United States, and Japan that did not adequately meet Africa's cotton interests, it would have been inconceivable for the four African countries to block the deal.

They would have faced immense pressure—including threats of expulsion from the WTO—to abandon their demands. Poor countries (except India because of its population size and large pockets of wealth) remain quite marginalized at the WTO.

The second problem with the emancipation of the global middle class is that generalization of veto power is not a viable solution to the woes of the WTO. Ministers of six countries could not reach a very high-stakes agreement on July 24, 2006. Even if one resigned oneself to brush aside the very compelling demands on cotton, sugar, or textiles from the African continent, reaching unanimous agreement on a wide range of trade issues among a large and rising number of middle-income countries is just not going to be practical.

Some analysts propose to rely on alliances and a more-or-less formal system of constituencies to circumvent the veto problem. Informal coalitions have mushroomed: there are the G20, G33, and G110, all groups of poor and middle-income countries. The idea is twofold. On the one hand, small countries with similar interests could join forces and exercise their veto right jointly as they are not able to do it individually. On the other hand, the total number of veto-wielding negotiating parties could be reduced by having some countries representing others, again whenever they have similar interests. When they negotiated with the European Union and the United States in July 2006, Brazil and India were essentially representing all other poor and middle-income countries.

That route is a dead end, in my analysis. Brazil and India could use their influence among other poor and middle-income countries to block negotiations. China alone might veto a WTO round of negotiations in a not-so-distant future. But at the end of the day, representatives of these large member-states are accountable to their own electorate and vested interests only. As illustrated above in the case of cotton, coalitions of poor countries or small middle-income countries would remain unable to exercise veto power on their own. More importantly, such coalitions would be unlikely to hold together, or would do so only around a very few symbolic negotiating positions. For each member of the WTO has very specific national economic interests. The United States and the European Union would find it easy to circumvent a coalition's potential veto through a divide-and-rule strategy by offering just enough concessions to some members of the coalition. Besides, the very legitimacy of a constituency system, by which one country would represent the interests of others at the negotiating table, is quite questionable. The WTO deals with virtually all aspects of economic policy, and I do not see how states would accept outsourcing their policy making to other governments, even ones with more or less similar interests.

Strong confederations just cannot function with many member-states. The WTO could function as long as only few member-states (the Quad) could exercise their veto right. It is unlikely to survive in an era where more member-states assert their veto power, either individually or as part of shifting coalitions. The multiplicity of issues and interests at stake, both national and transnational, make negotiations among a large number of players very difficult. Lack of legitimacy is therefore not the only reason to call for institutional reform. Multilateralism will probably die from paralysis.

A T THE TIME OF writing, the Doha Development Round remained at an impasse, and the WTO was at a critical juncture as an institution. As Lamy declared, the absence of a deal meant that everyone was a loser. That the middle class is now able to stop the excesses of the upper class does not make global trade policy making democratic. Global democracy entails that the middle class should be able to outvote the upper class and roll back some of its privileges. That is out of question in the short term. In the long run, several scenarios can be imagined.

A first scenario is that the suspension of talks at the WTO would last for several years. The United States and the European Union would continue with some success their divide-and-rule strategy of negotiating trade agreements outside of the WTO framework. The Bush administration in particular has been pursuing such a strategy aggressively by negotiating regional or bilateral trade agreements with those poor and middle-income countries that are most eager to access the American market at any cost. This strategy is a way to isolate countries that are more demanding in the framework of WTO negotiations. For example, the United States has now passed two regional free-trade agreements in the Americas (the North American Free Trade Agreement with Canada and Mexico, and the Central American Free Trade Agreement) plus a bilateral free trade agreement with Chile, and it is actively negotiating a third regional agreement with Andean countries. Such a strategy significantly isolates the Mercosur trading block of Argentina, Brazil, Paraguay, Uruguay, and Venezuela, which has been pushing a more reformist agenda at the WTO.

However, true free traders do not like regional and bilateral agreements because they bind multinational companies in a huge amount of red tape. Transactions between any two pairs of countries could eventually be subject to different trade regulations, defeating the purpose of free-trade zones. Under the first scenario, the pro-free-trade global economic elite would therefore fight back. They would concentrate their effort on domestic interests in the United States and Europe, particularly agribusiness, which has been the primary culprit for the failure of the Doha Round.

Reactions to the suspension of the round by free traders, articulated in the editorials of the *Wall Street Journal*, the *Financial Times,* or the *Economist*, attest of their concern about the future of globalization itself. Some free traders write about the first era of economic globalization, which stretched from the late nineteenth century to 1914, and involved the opening of large swaths of the world to the global market through colonization, with extensive freedom of movement of capital, goods, and workers. That era ended in a nationalist backlash of two world wars and a high degree of protectionism. As signs of protectionist sentiment are rising in Europe and America because the middle class does not benefit enough—and indeed loses—from globalization, the pro-free-trade elite's fear of history repeating itself is palpable. It is likely to increase during an extended suspension of talks at the WTO.

Nevertheless, American and European vested interests are not the only obstacles the pro–free-trade elite would face. Demands of Brazil, India, and China would remain on the table. With time, these countries would presumably become more powerful, barring possible financial crises stalling their economic growth. The combination of their rising clout and a prolonged stalemate at the WTO could lead them to reorient their positions further toward renationalization of economic management through the introduction of more extensive authorized opt-out rights.

Meanwhile, the influence of progressive global civil society shows no signs of abating either. As discussed in Part I, progressive groups have already scored victories in increasing transparency of information and accountability of intergovernmental organizations, and in securing their own participation in policy deliberations. Civil society groups scrutinize negotiations and advance their own proposals. The quality of information they produce helps the poorest countries, which do not have sufficient staff to analyze all the policy options under consideration at the WTO. They also mobilize the general public throughout the world, and have given voice to people who feel left out by globalization, from African cotton farmers to American blue-collar workers. Adding an explicit call for political equality in the form of equal universal suffrage at the WTO would help civil society put the pro-free-trade global elite even more on the defensive because there is no argument against equal universal suffrage. Progressive civil society may disagree with free traders on trade policy itself, but nobody opposes democracy as such.

Finally, free traders would also continue to face the WTO's archaic decision-making institutions, rendering negotiations ever less practical. In the medium term, Brazil, India, and China would be likely to consolidate their informal veto capacity. With the pro-free-trade global elite on the defensive, they could eventually manage to complete the Doha Development Round with a modest deal rolling back some of the rigged rules and double standards set in previous agreements by the United States and the European Union. For instance, they could obtain reductions in trade-distorting agricultural subsidies. The deal would otherwise mark a pause in the decades-long effort to open national markets to global competition. But a business-as-usual scenario that would simply add Brazil, China, and India to the Quad could not represent a permanent solution. Soon enough middle-sized countries like Mexico, South Africa, and South Korea would claim their own franchise. And the pressure of civil society for a WTO parliament with real power would gain momentum.

Eventually, the global elite would realize that saving globalization would require streamlining the WTO decision-making process and democratizing it so as to include those who feel left out. A formal amendment to the WTO statutes would ensue, taking a first step toward equal universal suffrage. For instance, a parliament directly elected by the member-states' populations could be instituted, which, in further incremental steps, could eventually share full decision-making power with the Ministerial Meeting, which is the assembly of representatives of national governments. Both organs would make decisions at a simple majority, the former according to the "one person, one vote" rule and the latter "one state, one vote." As a compromise, a very few number of states (e.g., the United States, the European Union, Japan, China, and India) could gain a formal veto right, which they would find increasingly hard to exercise as the idea of global democracy would over time become entrenched in everybody's view of the world. (Ironically—and in contrast with the experience of nineteenth-century Britain—the concept of political equality is already so entrenched today that intermediate voting systems including explicit privileges for a few member-states might prove politically difficult to introduce.)

At this time it is preposterous to imagine the U.S. Congress ratifying amendments to a trade agreement passed at the WTO despite a negative vote of the U.S. trade representative. But several decades is a long time, during which economic power relations are likely to change. For example, China's national income might equal that of the United States by 2040. This time could be used to anchor the simple idea that "every human being ought to have equal say in decisions that affect all humankind." Even most Americans could eventually recognize the legitimacy of a WTO parliament to which they themselves send representatives.

Nevertheless, this optimistic scenario is by no means the only possible one. The 1914 scenario is also plausible. The Doha Development Round could languish long enough to allow for the entrenchment of protectionism in the European Union and the United States as well as other major trading powers. Smaller countries that would not be able to rely on their domestic markets for sustained development would join small regional trading blocs, either linked to a rich trading power, like the Andean Free Trade Agreement, or not, like Mercosur. The WTO would fall into oblivion, and the deepening of economic globalization, through such efforts as adoption of more precise rules on trade in services or new rules on labor rights or competition policy, would never happen. In a more optimistic scenario, a few big regional trade areas would eventually regroup and agree on a modicum of rules to manage economic relations among themselves. In a darker scenario, economic nationalism would feed and be fed by fears of insecurity, driven by possible catastrophic terrorist attacks and proliferation of weapons of mass destruction. Exacerbated nationalism would eventually lead, maybe not to a third world war with nuclear holocaust, but at least to a new multipolar cold war, in which powerful countries like China, Iran, and the United States would wage wars by proxy in desolate regions.

There is also a third scenario combining elements of the first two. Just as I argued that the European Union could launch a new inclusive foreign policy that would eventually induce NATO reform, it could also develop global democracy by adopting a new approach to its own regional and bilateral trade agreements. Instead of negotiating trade agreements with poor and middle-income countries in a position of power in much the same way as the United States does, it could extend its internal global democratic institutions to its external trade relations.[24] The European Union already has so-called Economic Partnership Agreements with many of its member-states' former colonies in Africa, the Caribbean, and the Pacific. If Europeans really believed in building a just and peaceful world through international institutions, they should eventually be willing to share power fairly in the negotiation of such agreements, which means moving toward equal universal suffrage. That does not necessarily mean extending membership to the European Union itself to African countries, because Economic Partnership Agreements do not cover the full range of issues that the European Union legislates on. But it would mean extending freedom of movement of goods and services, and possibly extending the scope of authorized opt-out rights in the interest of poor countries. Regional trade agreements involving the European Union could then gradually expand geographically and set the tone for a resumption of global negotiations. For that matter, any other trading block could also adopt features of global democracy.

Before closing this discussion on trade, it is worth exploring the roles of India and China in these scenarios. Due to their demographic weights and fast-paced growth, they are bound to gain influence in global trade policy. India is a fairly stable democracy. Its economic growth has been steady and has further potential. India is also one of the powerhouses of progressive global civil society. It is thus likely to play a leading role in the development of global democracy.

China's future is much more uncertain. It is not governed through representative democracy at this time and would therefore not fit a democratic WTO. China's economy has grown at an amazing pace, and one should worry about the sustainability of that growth. Financial imbalances are rife: housing bubble, state enterprises in the red, and overinvestment in some industries, all of which make the banking sector vulnerable. Some analysts describe China's economy as a "bicycle" economy: If growth were to slow down too much or too fast, it could collapse. And the Communist Party could collapse with it. Rapid growth is indeed the one source of legitimacy that the party can use to remain in power when the Chinese people are themselves increasingly enmeshed with the ideas of freedom and democracy that pervade the world they live in.

China could thus play either a positive or negative role in building global democracy. A financial crisis could bring the country to its knees at any time, opening the door to democratization and, after a few years of recession, it could spring back and join India in the struggle for global democracy. Or it could not get over its recession for many years due to political instability, secessionist terrorism, social unrest, and a collapse of the state, out of which a nasty authoritarian and nationalist regime could emerge, a little like the story of Russia in the 1990s, only worse. This scenario, quite likely, would be the surest route to the 1914 scenario discussed above, especially when it is combined with an ongoing clash of civilizations between the West and Islam and an enduring American nationalism. Alternatively, the Communist Party may succeed in steering the bicycle economy clear of potholes in the road, incrementally introducing political reform as the economy matures. In any event, a Communist dictatorship is unlikely to survive in the long run, and the lack of democracy in China today should therefore not in itself cast doubts about the long-term development of global democracy. (Besides, the WTO could democratize without China anyway, and keep it integrated into the global economy through separate trade agreements.)

What is the global democratic approach to global policies on international finance, migration, and foreign aid?

After this extensive discussion of the global democratic approach to the regulation of international movements of goods and services, I will now briefly examine other global policy areas relevant to the promotion of economic and social rights: regulation of international movements of capital, movements of people, and foreign aid.

As to the regulation of movements of capital, the competence over international finance is divided among a number of important intergovernmental organizations. The WTO is competent for global regulation of the financial services industry, but the International Monetary Fund, the Bank for International Settlements, and the Organization for Economic Cooperation and Development are also involved in that policy area. The most important aspect of the regulation of international finance, the management of exchange rates between the major currencies, is supposed to be a prerogative of the G7, the group of finance ministers and heads of state of seven countries that used to be the richest (Brazil has now overtaken Canada, and China has overtaken Britain, France, and Italy to become the world's fourth-largest economy). But the G7 actually prefers to let financial markets set these rates unhindered.

With the exception of the WTO and the International Monetary Fund, all these intergovernmental organizations are weak confederations and have selective memberships. Some, like the G7, do not even have legal status under international law and are merely formal networks of national governments. Most of their decisions take the form of codes and standards with which member-states have great latitude to comply in whole or in part. Given the nature of international finance, however, they generally do comply fairly well. For failure to comply can lead capital to migrate toward complying countries, so much so that even some middle-income countries that are not members of some of these selective organizations seek compliance to norms that they have not been able to influence. The International Monetary Fund in particular is widely regarded as the gatekeeper to private financial markets. Middle-income countries like South Korea, Brazil, and Argentina have in recent years repaid their debts to the fund with zeal (i.e., before term) in order to demonstrate their creditworthiness to private investors.

According to a global democratic approach, the regulation of international finance should be made in the same way as the regulation of international trade, with federalism and equal universal suffrage. The case for authorized opt-out rights is even stronger for the regulation of international finance, however, as evidence shows that different national circumstances call for different degrees of liberalization of movements of capital.[25] Countries should keep the choice between free movement of capital with floating exchange rates or restricted movement of capital with managed exchange rates for at least as long as a truly transnational set of global economic rules emerges from the WTO. Meanwhile, regional monetary unions, such as the West African Economic and Monetary Union or the European Monetary Union, would also be consistent with global democracy.

IN REGARD TO MOVEMENT of people or migration, it must first be noted that while emigration is currently recognized as a human right, immigration is not. Article 13 of the Universal Declaration of Human Rights states that "everyone has the right to freedom of movement and residence within the borders of each state" and "everyone has the right to leave any country, including his own, and to return to his country." But people do not have the right to enter another country, except for asylum in cases where they are persecuted in their own country. International law on migration, which mostly covers issues around asylum and refugees, repression of illegal immigration, but also labor rights, is consequently adopted exclusively under the weak confederation model: States may easily opt out of any commitments.

A universal right to immigration is obviously opposed by rich countries due to their nationals' fears of competition for jobs, as well as fears of increasing the cosmopolitan character of their societies. In my personal opinion, however, it is an anachronism. In the perspective of building a global community to let global democracy thrive, it is also a liability. Nevertheless, the right to immigration is not necessary to the practice of global democracy in an era where information and ideas can freely cross borders—and where people do travel and even migrate a lot. After all, although Europeans do have the right to migrate within the European Union, only a small proportion of people actually exercise that right. Yet Europeans do practice global democracy on their continent.

According to global democracy, the right to immigration would become a legally binding human right only when a core group of countries throughout the world would voluntarily decide it to be so. They could set up an intergovernmental organization that would regulate immigration among themselves, according to the features of global democracy presented in Chapter 12. Note, however, that the WTO may assert itself competent for some immigration matters by stealth, through amendments to the existing General Agreement on Trade in Services. That trade agreement sets some general principles about cross-border provision of services, some of which require movement of people: It is not possible to import a haircut without importing the barber. The agreement is still in its infancy, though, as WTO members are simply invited to make concessions to each other in that area.[26]

THE FINAL SET OF global public policies relevant to the promotion of economic and social rights is foreign aid, and more particularly economic development aid (foreign aid also includes military aid). Development aid has two distinct objectives: increasing poor people's access to essential social services, and promoting economic growth in poor countries. Effective national economic policies supported by fair international trade rules are the main policies to achieve the latter objective, and foreign aid is only a complementary instrument. But given that governments of poor countries are cash-strapped, development aid is essential to meet the former objective.

Access to essential social services such as basic education, basic health care, and drinking water are already recognized as human rights. The international community has the duty to fulfill these rights, and the latest expression of that responsibility is the United Nations' Millennium Development Goals, a set of tangible targets to reduce poverty and increase poor people's access to essential social services.[27] The problem with the Millennium Development Goals is that all member-states of the United Nations share collective responsibility to meet them, but no one faces any specific responsibilities or incentives to contribute to them. Although national governments of poor countries bear primary responsibility to fulfill their citizens' rights, there is an explicit understanding that they cannot afford it, but there are no specific obligations for rich countries to help them. That is an institutional failure. A global democratic approach to the provision of essential social services would clarify accountabilities.

Aid distributed by intergovernmental organizations is currently raised according to an extreme form of weak confederalism: Donor countries give whatever they want (in other words, they may opt out of any contribution that is higher than what they are ready to pay). That is obviously also the case for bilateral aid (i.e., aid given by one state to another without passing through intergovernmental organizations). The only drivers of contributions are moral and peer pressure, not needs. Accordingly, the amounts given remain insufficient to provide the essential social services to which all human beings are entitled. Contributions ranged from 0.15 percent of national income by the United States to 0.92 percent by Norway in 2003.[28] Moreover, donor countries define the terms under which aid is disbursed. These terms are often tainted by national or special interests of donor countries, which reduces the effectiveness of aid in terms of poverty alleviation.[29] For example, a lot of aid is directed to poor countries according to geopolitical interests instead of needs (hence Egypt and Pakistan are major aid clients of the United States); and a large proportion of foreign aid benefits consultants of the donor country instead of poor people.

The global democratic approach to foreign aid for essential services would be to restrict opt-out rights. States that have recognized particular essential social services as human rights (e.g., elementary education from age six to fifteen, a certain amount of clean water per person per day, a basic health-care package) should be ready to pay for them in proportion to their financial means (e.g., gross domestic product). Once enough money is made available through binding contributions, recipient countries could be held accountable to provide the services to their citizens, and aid could be decreased if they failed to deliver the services with standard quality. The overall cost of meeting current commitments would imply increasing aid, but contributions would remain quite affordable according to United Nations estimates.[30]

By contrast, foreign aid aiming at fostering economic growth in poor countries could continue to rely solely on voluntary contributions. Such aid finances things like economic infrastructure (e.g., transportation, telecommunication), programs aimed at developing particular industries (e.g., agriculture, mining, tourism), or advice on economic policies. Abject poverty is a violation of human rights, but there is no right to economic equality. Even if one could estimate the impact of foreign aid on the speed of income convergence between poor and rich countries (current studies seem to show that there is no impact at all), there is no normative framework for determining what that speed ought to be.

IN SUMMARY, THERE ALREADY exists a far-reaching array of global economic policies about international trade and finance, migration, and foreign aid that affect most economic transactions in most countries. They are largely shaped by the national governments of rich countries, and are consequently tailored to the national interests of these countries. Not only is this unfair from the perspective of the nationals of poor countries, but it also impedes intergovernmental organizations from pursuing their stated objectives, which include the alleviation of global poverty. Global democracy would not necessarily transfer additional competences from the national to the global level of government—and could even transfer some back—but it would redistribute power at the global level in order to level the playing field among global economic actors and better align decision-making processes with the ultimate goal of poverty alleviation.

Global democracy is already making progress, thanks to a burgeoning global civil society and the increased clout of populous countries experiencing rapid economic growth, such as Brazil, China, and India. Due to these pressures, multilateralism is at a crossroads in the global economic policy area, and the future is likely to give birth to full-fledged global democracy, or to a return to nationalism.

16

Protection of the Global Environment

IN GENERAL TERMS, THE global democratic approach to global environmental policy is simply to let the world population decide the adequate level of protection of the global environment, based on majority rule with equal universal suffrage (one person, one vote). All the other institutional features of global democracy listed in Chapter 12 are relevant, and can be applied to the environmental policy area in the same manner as to the economic policy area developed in Chapter 15.

There are, however, a couple of differences between the environmental and economic policy areas that bear upon the way global democracy could develop. The first one concerns the allocation of competences across levels of government. Environmental protection is the one policy area for which the subsidiarity principle really can generate consensus about the allocation of competences across levels of government, as most environmental issues are intrinsically bound to specific territories. The management of a pond is clearly best dealt with at the municipal level. That of a river that crosses five states is best dealt with by an ad hoc intergovernmental organization of which these five states would be members.

Such reasoning leaves only the so-called global commons as areas of competence for global intergovernmental organizations. The global commons include oceans (currently regulated by the Law of the Sea), the atmosphere (currently regulated by treaties such as the Vienna Convention on the Protection of the Ozone Layer and the Framework Convention on Climate Change), outer space, and Antarctica (regulated by the Antarctic

Treaty). While different people have very different opinions about what constitutes adequate regulation of the global commons, at least one important part of the debate—that global commons are a matter of global interest to be dealt with by global intergovernmental organizations—is less controversial.

That said, there are also some environmental issues for which interpretation of the subsidiarity principle is contested. Biodiversity is a prime example. On the one hand, all states have the right to dispose of their natural resources, which suggests a limited role for international institutions in biodiversity conservation. Considering the colonial history of plunder of natural resources, environmental activists of rich countries should not lightly discard that important principle of international law. On the other hand, the whole humanity has an interest in conserving as many life forms as possible, which implies a duty on the part of the states that host endangered species.

As was the case with the other global policy areas, the transfer of competences on environmental policy from the national to the global level should be made freely by states signing treaties and joining intergovernmental organizations. In the case of biodiversity, poor countries with rich biological resources would obviously be more willing to join treaties that reward them for conserving resources than treaties that punish them for depleting them. If biodiversity has value for the international community, the international community should be ready to pay for it.

The second distinction of global environmental policy is the prevalence of the free-rider problem. A free-rider problem is a situation where each country has an interest in opting out of (or free riding on) a given global public policy, but is harmed by others opting out, too. For example, each country has an interest in not abiding by emission reduction targets for greenhouse gases because such reductions can harm the country's economy; but, at the same time, each country is harmed by others not reducing their own emissions either because it means global warming will continue apace with all the environmental consequences entailed for everyone.

Free-rider problems are a major reason why intergovernmental organizations are needed in the first place: to hold each state accountable for its actions. They are prevalent in all policy areas but especially in the environmental one. In particular, it is because of the potential for free riding that a World Environment Organization modeled after the World Trade Organization would be unlikely to function well. The institutional feature that has made the World Trade Organization so effective at generating and enforcing far-reaching economic regulations is that member-states must abide by all its trade agreements. In other words, opting out of specific agreements is not an option; only secession from the whole bundle is. What holds the World Trade Organization together is that the economic isolation that secession would entail can be very detrimental to national economic development. Due to the free-riding problem, a World Environment Organization would not have the same glue. To the contrary, states would face a very strong incentive to secede from it. Nothing could be better than isolation from strong global environmental rules: The rest of the world would take care of protecting the environment, but the seceding states would not bear any costs.

The institutional feature of global democracy that can help address free-riding problems is generalism (feature 9). Instead of creating a separate World Environment Organization modeled after the World Trade Organization, other existing or new intergovernmental organizations should venture in the environmental policy area. For example, the World Trade Organization itself could create environmental treaties or amend some of its existing treaties with environmental clauses. States would be induced to adopt such environmental regulations not because they like them but because they would want to remain members of the World Trade Organization.

This proposal is already being advocated by some environmentalists, but it is resisted by governments of poor countries. Given the imbalance of power between rich and poor countries at the World Trade Organization, the latter understandably fear that the former would impose environmental regulations that poor countries deem unaffordable. However, if the World Trade Organization were democratized, that problem would be solved. Instead of having to accept environmental regulations imposed on them by rich countries, poor countries would have the power to trade off environmental regulations in exchange for more favorable trade relations. Likewise, environmental regulations could be added to defense treaties, or to treaties defining universal rights to social services.

Straying from the environmental policy area as such, it is worth presenting the ninth feature of global democracy, generalism, in more depth. It is an important concept not only to address the free-rider problem, but also to guarantee that global democracy is fully achieved. As long as some global public policy-making forums remained undemocratic, they could vitiate the democratic forums because powerful states could bear upon the votes of weak ones in democratic intergovernmental organizations in exchange for favors in the organizations that would not be democratic.

For example, let us assume that the World Trade Organization were democratized but that the Security Council remained unchanged. China could exert undue influence at the World Trade Organization vis-à-vis a particular state by threatening to use its veto right at the Security Council in a situation that concerned that state. Or the United States could buy influence at the World Trade Organization by providing some states with bilateral security guarantees. Such power politics would disappear if global security were also dealt with in a global democratic way: As the weaker state would benefit from a strong security guarantee thanks to a global democratic defense alliance, it would not be subject to Chinese or American influence and could exercise its vote at the World Trade Organization in full independence.

Going a step further, there would be some value in having a single global democratic intergovernmental organization dealing with all global public policy areas, like the European Union more or less does at the regional level of government in Europe. The added value is the ability to expand negotiation opportunities across policy areas. In case negotiations on a particular set of global public policies, like regulation of trade in services, are stalled, opening them to another policy area, such as regulation of agricultural trade, allows for win-win agreements. Such cross-issue bargaining is already essential at the World Trade Organization. But the same principle would be relevant beyond trade. Expanding trade negotiations to environmental issues could expand the opportunities for win-win deals.

That said, institutional diversity also has value as it spurs innovation and is more flexible to accommodate diverse interests. Again, the European continent offers an example of that, as the European Union, albeit a general intergovernmental organization, is only one of a variety of intergovernmental organizations in Europe. The Council of Europe, the North Atlantic Treaty Organization, and the Organization for Security and Cooperation in Europe all have a role to play.

The transnationalization of world politics would also greatly facilitate decision making in the environmental policy area. I argued that a global parliament directly elected by the people was not absolutely necessary to global democracy, as national governments are representative of their people. However, representatives of constituencies of roughly equal size and smaller than most countries (e.g., one million inhabitants by constituency) would more readily represent transnational interests. Representatives of constituencies generally favorable to global environmental protection could coalesce regardless of their nationalities. If they represented a majority of the world population, they could pass strong protection measures even if constituencies against such protection happened to be concentrated in a few powerful countries, of which the national governments would presumably be opposed to strong protection. Obviously, if constituencies favorable to strong environmental protection did not represent a majority of the world population, transnational alliances would not help the environment. But that would be a normal outcome of democracy.

THE GLOBAL DEMOCRATIC APPROACH to global environmental policy could be applied to climate change, an issue that is likely to remain at the top of the global political agenda for decades to come. Measures to mitigate climate change raise the typical difficult political trade-offs of environmental issues: short-term and tangible economic costs borne by specific economic actors must be balanced with long-term and less tangible environmental and health benefits for the population at large. At the national or local levels of government, politicians often find it politically expedient to give greater consideration to the short-term costs and postpone action to protect the environment. The same would be true at the global level of government, even under global democracy.

There is, however, one way in which global democracy would significantly improve decision making on global environmental issues, and that is by addressing the free-rider problem. Both the costs and benefits of climate change, as well as the costs of mitigating climate change, vary widely across countries. Some countries face very high incentives to free ride on efforts to mitigate climate change. As long as negotiations take place among national governments that are supposed to defend national interests, in isolation from other global public policy issues, it will be very difficult to overcome the collective action problem.

The costs of climate change are predicted to be greater for countries around the tropics—generally poor countries. Some countries near the poles, such as Canada and Russia, could actually benefit from warmer weather. By contrast, the distribution of the costs of reducing emissions to mitigate climate change would greatly depend upon the way emissions are regulated. Under the Kyoto Protocol, rich countries have chosen a rule that suits them: Countries can emit an amount of greenhouse gases based on historical emissions—those who polluted most in the past are allowed to pollute most in the future. Such a rule is obviously unacceptable to poor countries: Economic development would lead them to pollute more in the future than they did in the past, such that committing to keep their emission levels flat would be prohibitively expensive for them. As a result of this manifest inequity, rich countries have agreed to let poor countries free ride for now: The Kyoto Protocol includes binding emission limits only for rich countries. However, China, India, and other poor and middle-income countries are industrializing rapidly and becoming major polluters as well. A new grand bargain is needed, and as both the number and diversity of actors multiplies, it will prove to be even harder to strike a deal than it was when Kyoto was agreed (and later reneged on by several of its signatories, including the United States).

Ethicist Peter Singer proposes such a new grand bargain: Emissions should be limited in proportion to population.[31] In other words, each human being should be given an equal quota of emissions because human beings are equal. Rich countries would find themselves polluting significantly more than their quota would allow them, and they would have to buy quotas from poor countries, which would emit less than their quota allocations. That could potentially lead to a huge financial transfer from rich to poor countries. Needless to say, rich countries would not join such an agreement, however ethical it may be.

Between the two extremes of historical emissions and equal emissions per head, there are of course many possible alternative rules to distribute the burden of mitigating climate change. Each of them would be very hard to negotiate as long as negotiations remained confined to a Kyoto-style forum because such forums require consensus among a large number of very diverse national interests. For instance, Australia and China currently produce a lot of their energy from coal, which is the combustible contributing most to climate change. It would therefore be much more costly for them to reduce their emissions by a certain proportion than for most other countries with their respective income levels. They would therefore demand more lenient treatment, as Australia has done under Kyoto. Every country could bring idiosyncratic considerations to the table, opening the door to posturing and brinkmanship—Australia eventually reneged on its Kyoto commitment.

A decision would be made more easily if it took place within a global parliament dealing with environmental as well as other global public policies and making decisions by majority rule. The solution could take the form, for instance, of a global tax on greenhouse gas emissions, which would induce people and companies to emit less. The tax proceeds would not need to be raised and spent by an intergovernmental organization: Each state could levy the tax on its domestic companies and use the proceeds as it sees fit—to finance a reduction of its income tax, for instance. The only thing that would be global would be the uniform tax rate, to be set by the majority of the world population.

With such a tax, reductions in emissions would be proportional to current emissions, such that rich countries would bear most of the burden (but also benefit most from the tax proceeds). Representatives of poor constituencies, constituting a majority in the global parliament, would not have an interest in a very high rate because their constituents would also have to pay the tax. But as their constituents would by and large be among the likely primary victims of climate change, they would probably vote for a meaningful tax rate. As is the case in all parliaments, representatives would also make deals among themselves across a wide range of issues. Some representatives of poor constituencies might agree to a lower carbon tax in exchange for more favorable trade rules, for instance. Unlike Kyoto-style agreements that can, at best, be reached once in a decade, the global carbon tax rate could be adjusted regularly, changing every time a majority of representatives find it a little too low or a little too high.

Climate change is truly an issue of global interest in which every human being has a stake. There is a way to deal with it efficiently that would content a majority of the world population. Shifting the negotiation setup from national constituencies to transnational ones would open up more options, like a flat tax, to deal with climate change and would facilitate decision making.

IN SUMMARY, THE GLOBAL democratic approach to global environmental policy essentially consists of letting the majority of the world population set global environmental rules. Global environmental policy making would function in the same way as global economic policy making, except that global environmental rules would better be bundled with other global rules, such as security guarantees, foreign aid, or trade privileges, in order to overcome the free-rider problem.

Conclusion

THERE IS NO GREATER power than an idea whose time has come. By the end of this century, the idea that all human beings ought to have equal say in decisions that affect all humankind is likely to be as commonplace as today's consensus that blacks are equal to whites, women to men, manual workers to CEOs. And today's nationalists are likely to be looked upon in the same way that we look back upon nineteenth-century imperialists.

Global democracy lies in the logic of millennia of human political development. However, human development does not follow a linear path. On many occasions, history has taken bypasses and detours. Dark ages separated the birth of democracy in Athens and its modern kind in Western Europe. Our world is susceptible to fall back into the dark ages again. Today's obscurantism is called nationalism. It is alive and well throughout the world. It is particularly scary in big powers like China, Japan, Russia, and the United States. Nationalist fervor feeds on its own growth, as one country's sentiments are aroused by similar sentiments abroad. "All you have to do is tell them they are being attacked, and denounce the pacifists for their lack of patriotism and exposing the country to danger. It works the same for every country," explained Herman Göring during his trial.[1] Nationalism feeds on fear, which tends to have the edge over hope. We are on the verge of cementing a new cold war, the West versus Islam, which would lead to further social unrest and restrictions on civil liberties, more catastrophic terrorism, and new asymmetrical interstate wars. Meanwhile, arms races and dangerous posturing among China, Japan, the two Koreas, India, Pakistan, Russia, and the United States could further erode the capacity of multilateral organizations to manage globalization, and could even escalate into major armed conflicts. It will therefore take courage for civil rights activists and politicians to build global democracy. I am an optimist and I believe that, with tenacity, progress will prevail. But all of us face a choice.

To guide that choice and close this book, I put forward take-away lessons for five different audiences: activists of the global movement for social justice, government officials of poor and middle-income countries, European federalists, American neoconservatives, and American Democrats.

FOR THE ACTIVISTS OF the global movement for social justice, I propose four lessons. First, institutions matter. Human rights, environmentalist, antipoverty, and peace activists have been using moral suasion to press politicians to transcend national interests and exercise leadership for the common good of the planet. Good arguments and popular mobilization have worked, to a degree. Yet at the end of the day, politicians are accountable to their national electorates. The pursuit of national interests is hardwired in current international institutions. Only radical institutional reform could produce a political environment that sustains good global solutions to global problems.

Activists of the global movement for social justice should recognize and reject the "governance without government" paradigm that currently shapes the views of reform-minded politicians. Some global problems can be solved through active citizen participation, without necessarily relying on intergovernmental organizations. But not all of them can, and typically not the most important ones, like nuclear proliferation for instance. Transparency, accountability, and participation are not substitutes for representation and equal universal suffrage. They are complementary. The electoral process, however insufficient it may have proved to be at the national level of government, must be replicated at the global level.

Second, activists of the global movement for social justice should develop a solid vision for global democracy. I have sketched one such vision. It is based on concepts familiar to national government that could be transposed with some flexibility and diversity at the global level. I hope that the rigorous conceptual battery I developed in this book will help others gauge their own visions. Proposals to reform intergovernmental organizations emanating from the movement are indeed too often tainted with wishful thinking. They are rarely tested with a cold analysis of how the proposed institutions would respond to self-interested actors pursuing national and transnational interests. Localists in particular should ponder the real tension that exists between devolution of authority to the national or local levels of government on the one hand, and the pursuit of universal human rights and other global goals on the other.

Many proposals for institutional reforms emanating from progressive authors tend to mix institutional reform itself and reform of global economic policy.[2] The idea is that true democracy cannot be reduced to civil and political rights. It also takes economic and social empowerment of poor and marginalized people to ensure that everyone can actually participate in the democratic process. I embrace that idea. Yet I believe that the global movement for social justice may be missing a big opportunity. No one is against civil and political rights. Despite the enormous interests at stake, promoting global civil and political rights should not be very difficult. For sure, it will take time and will require tenacity to challenge people's misconceptions about the global level of government, and to make Westerners come to terms with the fact that their values of civil and political rights imply the need for them to share power. But the basic argument is essentially won already. However, when calls for civil and political rights are mixed with demands for particular economic or security policies (such as a Tobin tax on international capital flows, for instance), opponents of such policies get an easy way to ignore the calls for civil and political rights.

At the end of the day, democracy does not imply protectionism or pacifism. A true democratic vision should allow for changes in the party in power and a variety of economic and security policies. I am not proposing that activists of the global movement for social justice reduce their efforts to promote economic and social rights. But I am proposing that they strategically advance an agenda for civil and political rights in parallel with, but with some distance from, such efforts. Exposing the illegitimacy of intergovernmental organizations with greater clarity and strength will put those in power on the defensive and foster their acceptance of economic and other global policy reforms. The promotion of civil and political rights will thus go hand in hand with that of economic and social rights, the former pulling the latter, and the latter reinforcing the former.

Third, activists of the global movement for social justice should escalate the rhetoric about global democracy. Messages about global democracy could easily be woven into all communications on global public policy issues, be they about human rights, trade, climate change, or the war in Iraq. Global democracy is a big idea that is astonishingly easy to communicate: "We believe that all human beings should have equal say in decisions that affect all of them." "The World Trade Organization is not democratic and that is not OK." "World Bank staff sometimes criticize our own lack of legitimacy; let's organize a global election to see who really represents the people." "The Security Council does not have proper checks and balances; that's bad in national politics, it's also bad in world politics." Such statements would of course invite rebuttals, but I hope that this book has shed some conceptual clarity to rebut the rebuttals with fairly simple analogies and examples.

Perhaps the simplest way to promote global democracy in day-to-day communications is to refer to intergovernmental organizations like the United Nations or the World Trade Organization as "our global government." I believe in the power of ideas, and also in the power of words. If activists of the global movement for social justice across the world used the phrase "our global government" on a routine basis, it would sooner or later be relayed by the mainstream press. And when ordinary citizens hear or read about their global government again and again and how undemocratic it is, they will eventually ask to elect their representatives.

Communicating about global democracy requires striking a fine balance between, on the one hand, real provocation to attract attention, force a debate, and challenge preconceptions, and, on the other hand, respect for the audience's self-esteem as well as connection with its values in order to avoid losing it. Further communication research is needed to refine communication about global democracy for various audiences, but

I suspect that emphasizing concrete abuses of power with a moderately passionate tone, and attacking the system—that is, the lack of check-and-balance mechanisms in world politics—rather than the people, could be powerful.

Fourth, the global movement for social justice needs to penetrate the global security policy area in earnest. The peace movement is much weaker than its equivalents for human rights, economic development and social justice, and the environment. It rises when Western troops are about to fire their first bullets—that is, when it is already too late—and falls when troops are withdrawn. The peace movement scored a big victory with the 2006 elections for U.S. Congress, but that was only due to the rising number of American casualties. It is far from clear at the time of writing that any long-term positive lessons will be drawn from the conflict in Iraq. Once the dust in Iraq settles, Americans are likely to support their commander in chief in further wars as long as the body count on their side is kept low, as has been the case in the past.

The peace movement direly lacks a credible long-term strategy. Tough short- and medium-term decisions must be made to deal with international terrorism, the proliferation of weapons of mass destruction, and other threats. The peace movement has surrendered that terrain to nationalist and benevolent imperialist think tanks. For example, I am not hearing anyone challenging Western politicians' claim that a nuclear Iran would be unacceptable. Pacifists prefer staying in their safety zone by claiming simultaneously that nuclear proliferation is indeed unacceptable, but that nonproliferation should be achieved through diplomacy and perhaps sanctions. Once diplomacy and sanctions fail (and the odds are that they will), it will be too late to challenge the premise that a nuclear Iran is unacceptable, and the warmongers are likely to have their way.

Global democracy has progressed much more in the areas of human rights, economic, and environmental policy. At best, further progress in those areas could support the development of global democracy in the security policy area as well. At worst, it would not take much for a serious deterioration of global security to further undermine intergovernmental organizations and wipe out the gains made in global democracy over the past fifteen years. Another catastrophic terrorist attack could trigger such a dynamic. All progressive campaigning organizations—from Amnesty International to Oxfam, from trade unions to grassroots women's groups—should reconsider their strategies in order to avert such a scenario. They are completely involved in world politics already anyway. They should abandon the false pretense that issues of war and peace are too political for them and therefore are to be avoided.

THE TAKE-AWAY LESSON FOR government officials of poor and middle-income countries is that they are essential spokespeople of global democracy. The burgeoning of global civil society will definitely continue to promote the idea that the time has come to share power in world politics. But in the end, officials of developing countries do represent their people; civil society does not. As long as the former are willing to play by the rules of an undemocratic global government, they offer ammunition to the opponents of global democracy.

The world needs leaders from poor and middle-income countries who are both courageous enough to defy Western powers (like Venezuela's President Chavez) and skillful communicators for a Western audience (very much unlike him). Opinion polls[3] confirm that Americans and Europeans are decent people who value fairness and support multilateralism essentially because they believe it is fair. No leader of the developing world is currently challenging that belief in a way that Americans and Europeans can understand. Brazil's President Lula da Silva comes perhaps closest to that description, and has developed a welcomed "South–South" diplomacy, forging alliances among poor and middle-income countries to increase their influence within intergovernmental organizations. However, neither da Silva nor any of his counterparts really questions the legitimacy of multilateralism.

Challenging the legitimacy of our global government is of course problematic for officials of poor and middle-income countries because, in the end, it is often in their interest to collaborate with it. Officials are exposed to the risk of condemning the diktat of our global government one day, and accepting that diktat the next day. Global democracy therefore raises a second communication challenge for officials of poor and middle-income countries: explaining to their electorates why they must both live with and rebel against an unfair global government. Officials of poor and middle-income countries must learn to portray world politics as a system of institutionalized inequality (which could be called an apartheid system). Institutionalized inequality is better than raw inequality or anarchy, but of course not as good as democracy. An organization like the World Trade Organization, for example, can be depicted as a glass half full or half empty: It yields better outcomes for poor and middle-income countries than bilateral negotiation processes in which nothing would mitigate the imbalances of power between rich and poor countries, but it is of course unjust by the democratic standard of equal universal suffrage. Hence, officials of poor and middle-income countries should find the right way to condemn the World Trade Organization in no uncertain terms in front of their electorate, while explaining why they should sign the next trade agreements it produces.

As the economies of some poor and middle-income countries develop rapidly, their officials also face the temptation of fostering nationalism. (In some countries, foremost China, the very idea of democracy is unwelcome—at least for now.) While they should continue to increase their power within and outside of intergovernmental organizations, they should also realize that balance-of-power politics will always remain a dangerous game that the West can play well. Pressing Western nations to follow their democratic ideal of democracy at the global level of government is the best way to avoid major violent confrontations, which are likely to be fostered by exacerbated nationalism in a more multipolar world.

THE TAKE-AWAY LESSON FOR European federalists is to do unto non-Europeans as they would do unto fellow Europeans. There is a fundamental dissonance between Europe's foreign policy toward the rest of the world and the foreign policy of European Union member-states toward each other. The former is based on multilateralism, the latter on global democracy. Multilateralism and global democracy both seek to ground international relations on strong institutions and the rule of law. But multilateralism does not rest on equitable power sharing. Europeans are overrepresented in most intergovernmental organizations thanks to the "one state, one vote" decision-making rule, and they exert much more influence than their representation suggests thanks to both their own economic power and the pivotal positions they adopt on many policy issues between the United States, on the one hand, and the rest of the world, on the other. It is therefore understandable that they like multilateralism. Moreover, thanks to its emphasis on the rule of law, multilateralism seems fairer than nationalism or benevolent imperialism. That helps Europeans cultivate their self-esteem, sometimes tainted with haughtiness, and wash their hands of American imperialism.

However, multilateralism is in the end little else than "imperialism light." It is to benevolent imperialism what oligarchy is to monarchy: government by a handful of powerful countries instead of a single one, the United States. The oligarchs consist of the United States, European countries, and sometimes other countries when and only when they wield power that makes them hard to ignore, as we have observed in recent years at the World Trade Organization. Oligarchy is indeed a little fairer than monarchy, but not fundamentally fair.

This book invites Europeans to fashion their foreign policy after the European integration itself. That could become the unifying foreign policy project that European federalists have long sought. Although equal universal suffrage is bound to decrease European formal power within our global government, advocating for global democracy could actually help Europeans gain significant legitimacy and thereby informal influence in world affairs for decades to come. Following a global democratic approach to peace and security, Europeans could exercise significantly more leadership in world politics despite their relatively weak defense capabilities. In the area of economic development and environmental protection, the European Union could continue its geographic expansion beyond Europe's borders, based on a more flexible, multilayered membership structure that would exclude new members from some policy areas like free migration or budget support while allowing core European members to continue deeper integration on their own. Such expansion would also increase the European Union's influence. More importantly, global democracy is simply the right approach to foreign policy, for reasons that European federalists know best.

THE TAKE-AWAY LESSON FOR American neoconservatives is that democracy is as important at the global level of government as it is at the national level. Their idea of a community of democracies—that the world will be a better place if all states adopt democratic institutions at the national level—is at odds with their faith in a powerful, unrestrained America and their suspicion of inclusive intergovernmental organizations. Implicit (and sometimes explicit) in that idea is that national democracies would be willing to accept global American leadership, or, in other words, become vassals of the United States. If vassal status is all there is on offer, one should not be surprised that proud nations like China or Iran prefer to remain "strategic competitors" or "states of concern," in other words, potential or actual enemies.

Mechanisms of checks and balances are very important at the global as well as national levels of government. While all states should be expected to pursue their national interests, the existence of an asymmetrically powerful state makes such mechanisms all the more important. Neoconservatives are nevertheless right to criticize our global government for its lack of effectiveness, its inertia, and the perils that such inertia can entail in a dangerous world.[4] But this inertia is due to ill-conceived checks and balances, such as pervasive opt-out rights in the human rights policy area or veto rights at the Security Council. It does not prove that all intergovernmental organizations are bound to be ineffective. Rather than further weakening existing intergovernmental organizations, neoconservatives should work toward democratizing them with the same enthusiasm as they have toward democratizing the Middle East.

Neoconservatives are right to defend American power as the ultimate factor of stability in the world, for example, as a dissuasion force against major would-be confrontations in Asia. But they should also recognize that power must be unleashed with legitimacy, and that power becomes legitimate only when it is shared. Encouragingly, the Iraq quagmire has already made several neoconservatives realize the danger of unchecked power.[5]

A decisive foreign policy able to deal with security threats effectively is not incompatible with democracy. Neoconservatives do support domestic democratic control over American foreign policy. But because we live in an interdependent world, where threats to American national security are threats to many other nations as well, and where American foreign policy can itself represent a threat to allies as well as declared enemies, neoconservatives should embrace global security policies controlled democratically by the nationals of all democratic states. In that way, global democracy can truly realize the neoconservative synthesis of pursuing idealist goals in the real world.

In May 2007, Senator John McCain laid out his foreign policy platform for the 2008 Presidential elections.[6] He made the doctrine of a community of democracies his own, calling for the creation of a League of Democracies, but emphasized that the United States ought to be ready to share power within that community. His platform can therefore be described as a synthesis of neoconservatism and multilateralism, something very similar to the global democratic approach I advocate in this book: let all the democracies of the world shape their foreign policies jointly. However, McCain was careful not to explain how his League would handle disagreements. At the end of the day, from Iraq and Iran to agricultural subsidies or climate change, disagreements are unavoidable, even among democracies, and even after thorough and respectful dialogue. Without majority voting with equal universal suffrage, McCain's League of Democracies is likely to fall into either the neoconservative camp (with the United States ending up taking unilateral action) or with multilateralists (accepting dangerous stalemates).

FINALLY, THE LESSON FOR American Democrats is that global democracy might be the foreign policy project that they have direly missed in past elections. The multilateral system put in place by Roosevelt and Truman and that generated high hopes and a surge of concrete results in the aftermath of the Second World War has long since lost its momentum—and left the Democrats without a foreign policy to speak of.[7] A President Gore or Kerry might have brought a more inclusive tone to Washington and would have been better received in foreign chancelleries, but they would have faced the same paralysis-prone system of multilateral cooperation at a time when paralysis had become not only unproductive but also dangerous. Presidential candidate Kerry attempted to come across as tough on defense, but the electorate preferred the real thing. His lack of decisiveness was not just a personal trait; it revealed the Democrats' lack of a foreign policy compass. While President Clinton got away with a security policy that could be characterized as reactive crisis management, that option lost its viability on September 11, 2001. As Democrats have won back Congress in 2006, their lack of a real foreign policy alternative is likely to become all the more apparent by 2008.

While on the face of it global democracy seems to be a foreign policy approach ill-suited to the United States, as it implies sharing power, it has some merits. First, as remarked above, the American public does value fairness and collaboration with other nations. With proper education on the failings of multilateralism—which should not be conceded to benevolent imperialists and nationalists alone—such attitudes could be translated, over a sufficient period of time, into support for global democracy.

Second, it is an intrinsically centrist approach, which offers hope for a better world that will speak to the liberal wing of the party, and at the same time allows room for decisive action to assuage the fears of the wider public. It incorporates the neoconservative criticism of multilateralism while recognizing its Achilles' heel of concentration of power.

Finally, global democracy is an incremental reform agenda that could stretch the endeavor of sharing power over several decades, thereby making it less threatening to the American public. Surely, it is not a platform for 2008. But by the middle of this century, it may well become the first choice of world politics.

Notes

Introduction

1. "America will never seek a permission slip to defend the security of our country." President George W. Bush, "State of the Union Address," Washington, DC, January 20, 2004, www.whitehouse.gov/news/releases/2004/01/.

2. "As president, I will not cede our security to any nation or to any institution, and adversaries will have no doubt of my resolve to use force if necessary. But I will always understand that even the only superpower on earth cannot succeed without cooperation and compromise with our friends and allies." Senator John Kerry, Speech delivered at the Council on Foreign Relations, New York, NY, December 3, 2003, www.cfr.org/publication.html?id=6576.

3. For a history of the franchise expansion in Britain, see "Elections in the United Kingdom," www.wikipedia.org/wiki/Elections_in_the_United_Kingdom#History.

4. Peter Singer, *One World: The Ethics of Globalization* (New Haven: Yale University Press, 2002), 145.

5. I would particularly recommend: Ann M. Florini, ed., *The Third Force: The Rise of Transnational Civil Society* (Tokyo: Japan Center for International Exchange and Washington, DC: Carnegie Endowment for International Peace, 2000); Michael Edwards and John Gaventa, eds., *Global Citizen Action* (Boulder, CO: Lynne Rienner, 2001); Jan Aart Scholte, *Democratizing the Global Economy: The Role of Civil Society* (Coventry:

Center for the Study of Globalization and Regionalization [University of Warwick], 2003).

6.　Florini, *Third Force*, 235.

7.　For a critical and systematic review of existing proposals to democratize international institutions, read Heikki Patomäki and Teivo Teivainen, *A Possible World: Democratic Transformation of Global Institutions* (London: Zed Books, 2004); For a recent blueprint of institutional reform emanating from a civil society forum, read Montreal International Forum, "Global Democracy: Civil Society Visions and Strategies," Report of the Global Democracy 2005 (G05) Conference, Montreal, Canada, May 29–June 1, 2005, www.g05.org.

Part I
Understanding Global Democracy

1.　Comprehensive studies of globalization include David Held, Anthony McGrew, David Goldblatt, and Jonathan Perraton, *Global Transformations: Politics, Economics and Culture* (Cambridge: Cambridge University Press, 1998); or Jan Aart Scholte, *Globalization: A Critical Introduction* (New York: Palgrave Macmillan, 2005). For global governance in particular, I propose the following general texts: Anthony McGrew, ed., *The Transformation of Democracy?* (Cambridge, UK: Polity Press, 1997); and Joseph S. Nye and John D. Donahue, eds., *Governance in a Globalizing World*, (Washington, DC: Brookings Institution Press, 2000).

2.　David Held, "Democracy and Globalization," in *Re-Imagining Political Community: Studies in Cosmopolitan Democracy*, edited by Daniele Archibugi, David Held, and Martin Köhler (Stanford: Stanford University Press, 1998), 22.

3.　Commission on Global Governance, *Our Global Neighborhood* (Oxford: Oxford University Press, 1995).

4.　A typical exposition of this argument can be found in Robert O. Keohane and Joseph Nye Jr., "Introduction," in Nye and Donahue, eds., *Governance*, 32–36.

5.　Oxfam International, *Beyond the Headlines: An Agenda for Action to Protect Civilians in Neglected Conflicts* (Oxford, UK: Oxfam International, 2003), www.oxfam.org/en/policy/briefingnotes/pp030916_headlines.

6.　Singer, *One World*, 150–95.

7.　The comparison between apartheid in the world and in South Africa was made by Troy A. P. Davis, *Appel pour une démocratie mondiale* [Call for World Democracy] (Paris: Desclée de Brouwer, 1998), 77–78. That comparison obviously has its limits, as at least the freedoms of speech and association are respected in the global apartheid.

8. Pippa Norris, "Global Governance and Cosmopolitan Citizens," in Nye and Donahue, eds., *Governance*, 155–77.

9. Anatol Lieven, *America Right or Wrong: An Anatomy of American Nationalism* (Oxford: Oxford University Press, 2004).

10. "The Great Constitutional Debate Begins," *Economist*, February 10, 2005.

11. Ronald J. Glossop, *World Federation? A Critical Analysis of Federal World Government* (Jefferson, NC: McFarland, 1993).

12. See Derek Heater, *World Citizenship and Government: Cosmopolitan Ideas in the History of Western Political Thought* (London: Macmillan Press, 1996); Joseph Preston Baratta, *The Politics of World Federation*, vol. 1: *United Nations, U.N. Reform, Atomic Control* (Westport, CT: Praeger, 2004); and Joseph Preston Baratta, *The Politics of World Federation*, vol. 2: *From World Federalism to Global Governance* (Westport, CT: Praeger, 2004).

13. James N. Rosenau and Ernst-Otto Czempiel, eds., *Governance without Government: Order and Change in World Politics* (Cambridge: Cambridge University Press, 1992).

14. This summary is based on James N. Rosenau, "Governance and Democracy in a Globalizing World," in Archibugi, Held, and Köhler, eds., *Re-Imagining Political Community*, 28–57.

15. Sanjeev Khagram, "Toward Democratic Governance for Sustainable Development: Transnational Civil Society Organizing around Big Dams," in Florini, ed., *Third Force*, 83–114.

16. Besides the extensive literature on civil society (see note 5), which includes numerous examples of public-private partnerships and multi-stakeholder processes, there is also an extensive literature on corporate social responsibility: Andrew W. Savitz, *The Triple Bottom Line: How Today's Best-Run Companies Are Achieving Economic, Social, and Environmental Success—And How You Can Too,* (San Francisco: Jossey-Bass, 2006); Christian Aid, *Behind the Mask: The Real Face of Corporate Social Responsibility* (London: Christian Aid, 2004), www.christian-aid.org.uk/indepth/0401csr/; "A Survey of Corporate Social Responsibility," *Economist*, January 25, 2005.

17. For the good reasons to bash pharmaceutical companies, visit Oxfam GB, "Health Papers and Resources," www.oxfam.org.uk/what_we_do/issues/health/papers.htm.

18. Global Stakeholder Panel 2020, *What NGO Leaders Want for the*

Year 2020: Report of the Second Survey of the Global Stakeholder Panel 2020, (Toronto, ON: 2020 Fund, 2004), www.kbs-frb.be/code/page.cfm?id_page=125&ID=437&Cnt=EN. This finding is corroborated by the proceedings of a seminar for civil society leaders on the subject of global democracy: Tony Fleming, Didier Jacobs, Heather Hamilton, Amelia Kucklewicz, James Riker, and Jan Aart Scholte, "The Challenge of Global Democracy: Report of a NGO Retreat Addressing the Democratic Deficits in International Decision-Making," Washington, DC, hosted by Oxfam America and Citizens for Global Solutions, December 3–5, 2003. See also Monitor Group, *NGO Engagement in International Governance: A Report from the Findings from a Survey and Interviews of Representatives of Civil Society and Intergovernmental Organizations* (London: Monitor Group, forthcoming).

19. James N. Rosenau, "Governance in a New Global Order," in *Governing Globalization: Power, Authority, and Global Governance*, edited by David Held and Anthony McGrew (Cambridge: Polity Press, 2002), 76.

20. Robert A. Dahl, *Democracy and Its Critics* (New Haven: Yale University Press, 1989).

21. Wolfgang H. Reinicke, *Global Public Policy: Governing without Government?* (Washington, DC: Brookings Institution Press, 1998), 100.

22. Reinicke, *Global Public Policy*, 221.

23. Rosenau, "Governance and Democracy in a Globalizing World," 39–40.

24. Thomas L. Friedman, *The Lexus and the Olive Tree* (New York: Farrar, Straus, Giroux, 1999).

25. See Ann Florini, *The Coming Democracy: New Rules for Running the World* (Washington, DC: Island Press, 2003), 190.

26. See note 5 to the Introduction for references containing many examples of ways in which transparency, accountability, and participation are fostered at the global level of government.

27. Quoted in Hetty Kovach, Caroline Neligan, and Simon Burall, "Power without Accountability?—The Global Accountability Report 1," (London: One World Trust, 2003), iv.

28. Florini, *Coming Democracy*.

29. Florini, *Coming Democracy*, 200.

30. Anne-Marie Slaughter, *A New World Order* (Princeton: Princeton University Press, 2004).

31. Slaughter, *New World Order*, 8.

32. "Tom DeLay's Chef d'oeuvre: A New Low in the Abuse of Electoral Rules for Partisan Advantage," *Economist*, October 16, 2003.

33. For a typology and bibliography of various approaches to global democracy, read James Riker, "Promising Visions and Strategies to Advancing Global Democracy," paper presented at the Global Democracy 2005 (G05) Conference, Montreal, Canada, May 29–June 1, 2005, www.g05.org.
34. Rosenau, "Governance and Democracy in a Globalizing World," 51.
35. Daniele Archibugi and David Held, eds., *Cosmopolitan Democracy: An Agenda for a New World Order* (Cambridge: Polity Press, 1995); Archibugi, Held, and Köhler, eds., *Re-Imagining Political Community*; and Held and McGrew, eds., *Governing Globalization*.
36. Held et al. *Global Transformations,* 449; Daniele Archibugi, "Principles of Cosmopolitan Democracy," in Archibugi, Held, and Köhler, eds., *Re-Imagining Political Community*, 217.
37. See Samuel S. Kim, *The Quest for a Just World Order* (Boulder, CO: Westview Press, 1984), 45.
38. For a good overview of the status of all nonsovereign territories in the world, see Global Policy Forum, "Nations & States: Lists Showing Complex Status," www.globalpolicy.org/nations/lists.htm.
39. For a more technical and thorough discussion of this topic, read Karel Wellens, ed., *International Law: Theory and Practice—Essays in Honor of Eric Suy* (The Hague: Martinus Nijhoff Publishers, 1998).

Part II
Choosing Global Democracy

1. "How do I respond when I see that in some Islamic countries there is vitriolic hatred for America? I'll tell you how I respond: I'm amazed. I'm amazed that there is such misunderstanding of what our country is about, that people would hate us. I am, I am—like most Americans, I just can't believe it. Because I know how good we are, and we've got to do a better job of making our case. We've got to do a better job of explaining to the people in the Middle East, for example, that we don't fight a war against Islam or Muslims. We don't hold any religion accountable. We're fighting evil. And these murderers have hijacked a great religion in order to justify their evil deeds. And we cannot let it stand." President George W. Bush, press conference, Washington, DC, October 11, 2001.
2. On Arab public opinion vis-à-vis the West, read James J. Zogby, *What Arabs Think: Values, Beliefs, and Concerns* (Utica, NY: Zogby International, 2002); Shibley Telhami, *The Stakes: America and the Middle East: The Consequences of Power and the Choice for Peace* (Boulder, CO: Westview

Press, 2002); and Advisory Group on Public Diplomacy for the Arab and Muslim World, "Changing Minds, Winning Peace: A New Strategic Direction for U.S. Public Diplomacy in the Arab and Muslim World," Report submitted to the Committee on Appropriations, U.S. House of Representatives, October 1, 2003.

3. "Poll Shows Growing Arab Rancor At US," *Washington Post*, July 23, 2004.

4. Charles Tripp, "Leçons d'une histoire coloniale oubliée" [Lessons of a forgotten colonial history], *Le Monde Diplomatique* (Paris), January 2003.

5. Michel Despratx and Barry Lando, "Notre ami Saddam: Quand les Etats-Unis et la France s'alliaient à la dictature" [Our friend Saddam: When the United States and France were allies of the dictatorship], *Le Monde Diplomatique* (Paris), November 2004.

6. On the pre-1991 atrocities of Saddam Hussein and the complicity of Western powers, read: Nezan Kendal, "Quand 'notre ami' Saddam gazait ses Kurdes" [When 'our friend' Saddam was gassing his Kurds], *Le Monde Diplomatique* (Paris), March 1998; Joe Stork, "Armer aujourd'hui, détruire demain: l'Iraqgate' ou le cynisme-roi" [Arm today, destroy tomorrow: The 'Iraqgate' or the reign of cynicism], *Le Monde Diplomatique* (Paris), February 1993; Robert Parry, "Iraqgate: Confession and Cover-Up," *Extra!* (Fairness and Accuracy in Reporting [FAIR]), May–June 1995, www.fair. org/index.php?page=1291; and Human Rights Watch, *Genocide in Iraq: The Anfal Campaign against the Kurds* (New York: Rights Watch, 1993).

7. "We've sent a message that is understood throughout the world: if you harbor a terrorist, if you support a terrorist, if you feed a terrorist, you're just as guilty as the terrorists, and the Taliban found out what we meant." President George W. Bush, "Remarks by the President to the 85th Annual American Legion National Convention," speech delivered at the St. Louis Convention Center, St. Louis, Missouri, August 26, 2003.

8. On the consequences of the sanctions against Iraq and the shared responsibility of Saddam Hussein and Western governments in them, see www.global-citizens.org.

9. Rahul Mahajan, "We Think the Price Is Worth It: Media Uncurious about Iraq Policy's Effects—There or Here," *Extra!* (FAIR), November–December 2001, www.fair.org/index.php?page=1084.

10. On American reporting about the Iraq sanctions, read Seth Ackerman, "New York Times on Iraq Sanctions: A Case of Journalistic Malpractice," *Extra!* (FAIR), March–April 2000, www.fair.org/index.php?page=1025; Jim Naureckas, "Wolf Blitzer for the Defense (Department): Making Sure the Official Line is the Last Word," *Extra!* (FAIR), January–February

2003, www.fair.org/index.php?page=1126; Seth Ackerman, "A Timely Scandal" Oil-for-Food Charges Conveniently Tarnish U.N.," *Extra!* (FAIR), July–August 2004, www.fair.org/index.php?page=1186; Fairness and Accuracy in Reporting, "For the *New York Times*, Iraq Deaths Are the Other Guy's Fault," *FAIR Action Alert*, August 6, 1999, www.fair. org/index.php?page=1773; Fairness and Accuracy in Reporting, "'Paper of Record' Distorts Record on Iraq Sanctions," *FAIR Action Alert*, September 13, 2000, www.fair.org/index.php?page=1722; and Fairness and Accuracy in Reporting, "Common Myths in Iraq Coverage," *FAIR Action Alert*, November 27, 2002, www.fair.org/index.php?page=1638. On reporting about the Baathist regime's atrocities, read Seth Ackerman, "The *Washington Post*'s Gas Attack: Today's Outrage Was Yesterday's No Big Deal," *Extra!* (FAIR), September–October 2002, www.fair.org/index. php?page=1121. By contrast, the main commercial television broadcaster in Britain, ITV, did broadcast a ninety-minute documentary condemning the Iraq sanctions on March 6, 2000: *Paying the Price: The Killing of the Children in Iraq* (by John Pilger). Martin Shaw published an interesting debate over that documentary on the Internet at www.sussex.ac.uk/Users/hafa3/iraq.htm. While it is always easy to point out the imperfections of a documentary, Shaw's conclusion that Pilger's documentary was overall a disservice to the Iraqi people is amazing given the dearth of critical reporting about this most important foreign policy issue over a ten-year period.

I have not seen any challenge of the two main arguments used by the U. S. government in the mainstream American press to justify the sanctions against Iraq. The first argument was that Saddam Hussein had the power to end the sanctions by fully cooperating with the United Nations on the issue of disarmament. That is an "ends-justify-the-means" argument. Yet the whole point of international humanitarian law is that there are practices that no policy objective can justify. The second argument was that Saddam Hussein was much worse to his people than the sanctions. Besides the fact that it is irrelevant to the United Nations and United States' own responsibilities, that statement is, unfortunately, arguable. Reasonable estimates of the toll of the sanctions, ranging from the deaths of one hundred thousand to half a million children under five years of age alone ("When Sanctions Don't Work," *Economist*, April 6, 2000), are of the same order of magnitude as the two most lethal campaigns that Saddam Hussein waged against his own people—the genocide of up to four hundred thousand Kurds between 1974 and 1991 and of several tens of thousands and perhaps more than one hundred thousand Shiites in 1991. It is particularly unsettling that the U.S. government would resort to "ends-justify-the-means" and "my-enemy-is-worse-than-me" arguments, given that its enemies justify their own atrocities in exactly the same way. In a videotaped address released soon after the attacks of September 11, 2001, Osama Bin Laden said: "What America is tasting now is something insignificant compared to what we have tasted for scores of years. Our nation [the Islamic world] has been tasting this humiliation and this degradation for more than 80 years. Its sons are killed, its blood is shed, its sanctuaries are attacked, and no one hears and no one heeds. [. . .] Millions of innocent children are being killed as I speak. They are being killed in Iraq without committing any sins, and we don't hear condemnation or a fatwa [religious decree] from the rulers. [. . .] When people at the ends of the earth, Japan, were killed by the hundreds of thousands, young and old, it was not considered a war crime, it is something that has justification. Millions of children in Iraq is something that has justification. But when they lose dozens of people in Nairobi and Dar es Salaam [capitals of Kenya and Tanzania, where U.S. embassies were bombed in 1998], Iraq was struck and Afghanistan was struck. Hypocrisy stood in force behind the head of infidels worldwide, behind the cowards of this age, America and those who are with it." Videotape of Osama Bin Laden, released on October 7, 2001, www.september11news.com/OsamaSpeeches.htm.

11.   Amnesty International, *Guantanamo and Beyond: The Continuing Pursuit of Unchecked Executive Power* (London: Amnesty International, May 2005), www.amnesty.org/library/Index/ENGAMR510632005; Human Rights Watch, *The Road to Abu Ghraib* (Washington: Human Rights Watch, June 2004), www.hrw.org/reports/2004/usa0604; Human Rights Watch, *Getting Away with Torture? Command Responsibility for Human Rights for the U.S. Abuses of Detainees* (Washington: Human Rights Watch, April 2005), www.hrw.org/reports/2005/us0405.

12.   Human Rights Watch, "'Enduring Freedom': Abuses by U.S. Forces in Afghanistan," (Washington: Human Rights Watch, March 2004), www.hrw.org/reports/2004/afghanistan0304.

13.   See Physicians for Human Rights, *Preliminary Assessment of Alleged Mass Gravesites in the Area of Mazar-I-Sharif, Afghanistan: January 16–21 and February 7–14* (Boston: Physicians for Human Rights, 2001), www.phrusa.org/research/afghanistan/report_graves.html#13. The recommendations for investigation of Physicians for Human Rights were never followed. See also

Jamie Doran, *Afghan Massacre: The Convoy of Death* [documentary film]; for information about the film, see ACFTV, "Afghan Massacre," www.acftv.com/archive/article.asp?archive_id=1.

14. Bob Woodward, *State of Denial: Bush at War, Part III* (New York: Simon & Schuster, 2006); Michael Isikoff and David Corn, *Hubris: The Inside Story of Spin, Scandal, and the Selling of the Iraq War* (New York: Crown, 2006); Thomas E. Ricks, *Fiasco: The American Adventure in Iraq* (New York: Penguin, 2006); and Francis Fukuyama, *America at the Crossroads: Democracy, Power, and the Neo-Conservative Legacy* (New Haven: Yale University Press, 2006).

15. On the Kosovo war, see www.global-citizens.org.

16. On the dynamic of Chinese and Japanese nationalism as it plays itself out today, read "China and Japan: So Hard to Be Friends," *Economist*, March 26–April 1, 2005, 23–25, and "In Dangerous Waters," *Economist*, October 7–13, 2006, 29–31.

17. On nationalism and militarism in the United States, read: Andrew J. Bacevich, *The New American Militarism: How Americans Are Seduced by War* (New York: Oxford University Press, 2005); Lieven, *America Right or Wrong*; and Philip S. Golub, "Dieu, la nation et l'armée, une sainte trinité" [God, Nation and Army: A Holy Trinity], *Le Monde Diplomatique* (Paris), July 2005.

18. On the lack of legitimacy of the war against Serbia over Kosovo in 1999, see www.global-citizens.org.

19. Johanna McGeary, "Freedom Fighters," *Time*, March 8, 1999.

20. International Forum on Globalization, *Alternatives to Economic Globalization: A Better World Is Possible* (San Francisco: Berrett-Koehler, 2002); Colin Hines, *Localization: A Global Manifesto* (London: Earthscan, 2000); and Patomäki and Teivainen, *Possible World*.

21. Oxfam International, *Rigged Rules and Double Standards: Trade, Globalization, and the Fight against Poverty* (Oxford, UK: Oxfam International, 2002). See also Oxfam International, "Make Trade Fair," www.maketradefair.com.

22. Frances Stuart and Sam Daws, "An Economic and Social Security Council at the United Nations," Queen Elizabeth House Working Papers Series, no. 68, Oxford University, 2001.

23. For an empirical study of bribery at the Security Council, read: Ilyanna Kuziemko and Eric Werker, "How Much Is a Seat on the Security Council Worth? Foreign Aid and Bribery at the United Nations," *Journal of Political Economy* 114, no. 5 (October 2006): 905–30.

24. Some of these features are briefly discussed in Didier Jacobs, "Democratizing Global Economic Governance," in *After Neoliberalism: Economic Policies that Work for the Poor—A Collection of Papers Presented at a Conference on Alternatives to Neoliberalism, May 23–24 in Washington, DC*, edited by Jim Weaver, Didier Jacobs, and Jamie Baker (Washington, DC: New Rules for Global Finance, 2003), available at www.new-rules. org/afterneoliberalism.htm.

25. Robert Kagan, *Of Paradise and Power: America and Europe in the New World Order* (New York: Alfred Knopf, 2003).

Part III
Applying Global Democracy

1. William E. Odom and Robert Dujarric, *America's Inadvertent Empire* (New Haven: Yale University Press, 2004), 217.

2. United Nations General Assembly, "2005 World Summit Outcome," document A/RES/60/1 (New York: United Nations, 2005), 30.

3. International Commission on Intervention and State Sovereignty, *The Responsibility to Protect: The Report of the International Commission on Intervention and State Sovereignty* (Ottawa: International Development Research Center, 2001).

4. On the Kosovo war, see www.global-citizens.org.

5. German Marshall Fund of the United States, "Transatlantic Trends," a project of the German Marshall Fund of the United States and the Compagnia di San Paolo, 2002, 2003, 2004, 2005, 2006, www. transatlantictrends.org.

6. Chicago Council on Foreign Relations, *Worldviews 2004: American Public Opinion and Foreign Policy* (Chicago: Chicago Council on Foreign Relations, 2004).

7. The Aspen Institute, *From Values to Advocacy: Activating the Public's Support for U.S. Engagement in an Interdependent World* (Washington, DC: Aspen Institute, 2002).

8. For a brief account of the state of European foreign and defense policy, read "Abroad Be Dangers: The European Union in the World," *Economist*, August 26–September 1, 2006.

9. "The Price of Peace," *Economist*, April 22, 2004, www.economist.com/ displayStory.cfm?Story_id=2592716.

10. Francis Fukuyama, "The End of History," *National Interest*, Summer 1989; Samuel Huntington, "The Clash of Civilizations," *Foreign Affairs*, 72, no. 3 (1993): 22–49.

11. See Archibugi, "Principles of Cosmopolitan Democracy."

12. For the case in favor of economic globalization, read for instance: Martin Wolf, *Why Globalization Works* (New Haven: Yale University Press, 2004). For the case against it, read for instance: Ralph Nader, et al., *The Case against "Free Trade": GATT, NAFTA, and the Rise of Corporate Power* (Berkeley, CA: North Atlantic Books, 2003).

13. Ha-Joon Chang, *Kicking away the Ladder: Development Strategy in Historical Perspective* (London: Anthem Press, 2002); Dani Rodrik, "The Governance of Trade as if Development Really Mattered," paper prepared for the United Nations Development Program, April 2001, Harvard University, Cambridge. For a similar argument but focusing on national regulation of capital flows, read Dani Rodrik, "Governing the World Economy: Does One Architectural Style Fit All?" in *Brookings Trade Forum: 1999*, edited by Susan Collins and Robert Lawrence (Washington, DC: Brookings Institution, 1999).

14. Chang, *Kicking away the Ladder*; Rodrik, "Governance of Trade."

15. Oxfam International, *Rigged Rules and Double Standards.*

16. See Oxfam International, *Rigged Rules and Double Standards,* and other policy briefing papers available at www.oxfam.org/eng/policy_pape.htm.

17. World Trade Organization, "Doha Declaration 2001," paragraph 4 (Geneva: World Trade Organization, 2001).

18. Oxfam International, *From Development to Naked Self-Interest: The Doha Development Round Has Lost Its Way* (Oxford, UK: Oxfam International, 2005), www.oxfam.org/eng/pdfs/bn050727_wto_development.pdf.

19. Singer, *One World*, 57–65.

20. Oxfam International, *Rigged Rules and Double Standards.*

21. Chang, *Kicking away the Ladder*; Rodrik, "Governance of Trade."

22. Dani Rodrik, "Governance of Economic Globalization" in Nye and Donahue, eds., *Governance*, 347–365.

23. On the rising power of "emergening economies," read "The New Titans: A Survey of the World Economy," *Economist,* September 16, 2006.

24. On the European Union's trade policy toward poor countries, read Oxfam International, Europe's Double Standards: How the EU Should Reform Its Trade Policies with the Developing World (Oxford, UK: Oxfam International, 2002), www.oxfam.org/en/files/pp0204_Europes_Double_Standards.pdf/download.

25. Weaver, Jacobs, and Baker, *After Neoliberalism*. On the impact of one-size-fits-all liberalization of international movements of capital on economic development of poor countries, read Oxfam America, *Global Finance Hurts*

the Poor: Analysis of the Impact of North-South Private Capital Flows on Growth, Inequality, and Poverty (Boston: Oxfam America, 2002).

26. On the potential of the General Agreement on Trade in Services to promote free migration, read Caroline Dommen, "Migrants' Human Rights: Could GATS Help?" *Migration Information Source* (Migration Policy Institute), March 1, 2005, www.migrationinformation.org/Feature/display.cfm?id=290.

27. United Nations, "Resolution Adopted by the General Assembly 55/2: United Nations Millennium Declaration," September 8, 2000, www.un.org/millennium/declaration/ares552e.htm. See also www.un.org/millenniumgoals/.

28. Oxfam International, *Paying the Price: Why Rich Countries Must Invest Now in a War against Poverty* (Oxford, UK: Oxfam International, 2004), www.oxfam.org/eng/pdfs/pp041206_MDG.pdf.

29. Oxfam International, *Paying the Price*, and Oxfam International, *In the Public Interest: Health, Education, and Water and Sanitation for All* Oxford: Oxfam International, 2004), www.oxfam.org/en/policy/briefingpapers/bp_public_internest.

30. Millennium Project, *Investing in Development: A Practical Plan to Achieve the Millennium Development Goals* New York: Millennium Project, 2005), www.unmillenniumproject.org/reports/fullreport.htm.

31. Singer, *One World*.

Conclusion

1. Quoted in Robert B. Reich, *Reason: Why Liberals Will Win the Battle for America* (New York: Vintage Books, 2004), 153.

2. This is apparent in the critical review of institutional reform proposals by Patomäki and Teivainen, *Possible World*, for instance.

3. See notes 5–7 in Part III.

4. Kagan, *Of Paradise and Power*.

5. See Andrew Sullivan, "What I Got Wrong about the War," *Time*, March 13, 2006; and Fukuyama, "End of History."

6. Speech on foreign policy delivered by Senator John McCain at The Hoover Institution on May 1, 2007. See also: "Concert of Democracies: A seductive sound," *Economist*, June 9, 2007.

7. George Packer, "A Democratic World: Can Liberals Take Foreign Policy back from the Republicans?" *New Yorker*, February 16–23, 2004.

Bibliography

Globalization

General texts

Held, David, Anthony McGrew, David Goldblatt, and Jonathan Perraton. *Global Transformations: Politics, Economics and Culture.* Cambridge: Cambridge University Press, 1998.

Scholte, Jan Aart. *Globalization: A Critical Introduction.* New York: Palgrave Macmillan, 2005.

Economic globalization

Friedman, Thomas L. *The Lexus and the Olive Tree.* New York: Farrar, Straus, Giroux, 1999.

Ha-Joon Chang. *Kicking away the Ladder: Development Strategy in Historical Perspective.* London: Anthem Press, 2002.

Nader, Ralph, et al. *The Case against "Free Trade": GATT, NAFTA, and the Rise of Corporate Power.* Berkeley, CA: North Atlantic Books, 2003.

Oxfam America. *Global Finance Hurts the Poor: Analysis of the Impact of North-South Private Capital Flows on Growth, Inequality, and Poverty.* Boston: Oxfam America, 2002.

Oxfam International. *Rigged Rules and Double Standards: Trade, Globalization, and the Fight against Poverty.* Oxford, UK: Oxfam International, 2002.

Rodrik, Dani. "Governing the World Economy: Does One Architectural Style Fit All?" In *Brookings Trade Forum: 1999*, ed. Susan Collins and Robert Lawrence. Washington, DC: Brookings Institution, 1999.

Rodrik, Dani. "The Governance of Trade as if Development Really Mattered." Paper prepared for the United Nations Development Program, April 2001, Harvard University, Cambridge.

Wolf, Martin. *Why Globalization Works.* New Haven: Yale University Press, 2004.

Global Governance

Governance without government

Florini, Ann. *The Coming Democracy: New Rules for Running the World.* Washington, DC: Island Press, 2003.

Nye, Joseph S., and John D. Donahue, eds., *Governance in a Globalizing World.* Washington, DC: Brookings Institution Press, 2000.

Reinicke, Wolfgang H. *Global Public Policy: Governing without Government?* Washington, DC: Brookings Institution Press, 1998.

Rosenau, James N. "Governance and Democracy in a Globalizing World." In *Re-Imagining Political Community: Studies in Cosmopolitan Democracy,* edited by Daniele Archibugi, David Held, and Martin Köhler, 28–57. Stanford: Stanford University Press, 1998.

Rosenau, James N. "Governance in a New Global Order." in *Governing Globalization: Power, Authority, and Global Governance,* ed. David Held and Anthony McGrew. Cambridge, UK: Polity Press, 2002.

Rosenau, James N., and Ernst-Otto Czempiel, eds. *Governance without Government: Order and Change in World Politics.* Cambridge: Cambridge University Press, 1992.

Slaughter, Anne-Marie. *A New World Order.* Princeton: Princeton University Press, 2004.

Cosmopolitan democracy

Archibugi, Daniele. "Principles of Cosmopolitan Democracy." In *Re-Imagining Political Community: Studies in Cosmopolitan Democracy,* edited by Daniele Archibugi, David Held, and Martin Köhler. Stanford: Stanford University Press, 1998.

Archibugi, Daniele, and David Held, eds. *Cosmopolitan Democracy: An Agenda for a New World Order.* Cambridge: Polity Press, 1995.

Held, David. "Democracy and Globalization." In *Re-Imagining Political Community: Studies in Cosmopolitan Democracy,* edited by Daniele

Archibugi, David Held, and Martin Köhler. Stanford: Stanford University Press, 1998.

McGrew, Anthony, ed. *The Transformation of Democracy?* Cambridge, UK: Polity Press, 1997.

World federalism

Baratta, Joseph Preston. *The Politics of World Federation.* Vol. 1, *United Nations, U.N. Reform, Atomic Control.* Westport, CT: Praeger, 2004.

Baratta, Joseph Preston. *The Politics of World Federation.* Vol. 2, *From World Federalism to Global Governance.* Westport, CT: Praeger, 2004.

Davis, Troy A. P. *Appel pour une démocratie mondiale* [Call for World Democracy]. Paris: Desclée de Brouwer, 1998.

Glossop, Ronald J. *World Federation? A Critical Analysis of Federal World Government.* Jefferson, NC: McFarland, 1993.

Heater, Derek. *World Citizenship and Government: Cosmopolitan Ideas in the History of Western Political Thought.* London: Macmillan Press, 1996.

Other perspectives on global governance and democracy

Dahl, Robert A. *Democracy and Its Critics.* New Haven: Yale University Press, 1989.

Fleming, Tony, Didier Jacobs, Heather Hamilton, Amelia Kucklewicz, James Riker, and Scholte, Jan Aart. "The Challenge of Global Democracy: Report of a NGO Retreat Addressing the Democratic Deficits in International Decision-Making." Hosted by Oxfam America and Citizens for Global Solutions, Washington, DC, December 3–5, 2003.

Jacobs, Didier. "Democratizing Global Economic Governance." In *After Neoliberalism: Economic Policies that Work for the Poor—A Collection of Papers Presented at a Conference on Alternatives to Neoliberalism, May 23–24 in Washington, DC,* edited by Jim Weaver, Didier Jacobs, and Jamie Baker. Washington, DC: New Rules for Global Finance, 2003. www.new-rules.org/afterneoliberalism.htm.

Monitor Group. *NGO Engagement in International Governance: A Report from the Findings from a Survey and Interviews of Representatives of Civil Society and Intergovernmental Organizations.* London: Monitor Group, forthcoming.

Montreal International Forum. "Global Democracy: Civil Society Visions and Strategies." Report of the Global Democracy 2005 (G05) Conference, Montreal, Canada, May 29–June 1, 2005. www.g05.org.

Patomäki, Heikki, and Teivo Teivainen. *A Possible World: Democratic Transformation of Global Institutions.* London: Zed Books, 2004.

Riker, James. "Promising Visions and Strategies to Advancing Global Democracy." Paper presented at the Global Democracy 2005 (G05) Conference, Montreal, Canada, May 29–June 1, 2005. www.g05.org.

Rodrik, Dani. "Governance of Economic Globalization." In *Governance in a Globalizing World*, ed. Joseph S. Nye and John D. Donahue, 347–65. Washington, DC: Brookings Institution Press, 2000.

Singer, Peter. *One World: The Ethics of Globalization.* New Haven: Yale University Press, 2002.

Corporate social responsibility

"A Survey of Corporate Social Responsibility." *Economist*, January 25, 2005.

Christian Aid. *Behind the Mask: The Real Face of Corporate Social Responsibility.* London: Christian Aid, 2004. www.christian-aid.org.uk/indepth/0401csr/.

Savitz, Andrew W. *The Triple Bottom Line: How Today's Best-Run Companies Are Achieving Economic, Social, and Environmental Success—And How You Can Too.* San Francisco: Jossey-Bass, 2006.

Global civil society

Edwards, Michael, and John Gaventa, eds. *Global Citizen Action.* Boulder, CO: Lynne Rienner, 2001.

Florini, Ann M., ed. *The Third Force: The Rise of Transnational Civil Society.* Tokyo: Japan Center for International Exchange and Washington, DC: Carnegie Endowment for International Peace, 2000.

Kovach, Hetty, Caroline Neligan, and Simon Burall. "Power without Accountability?—The Global Accountability Report 1." London: One World Trust, 2003.

Scholte, Jan Aart. *Democratizing the Global Economy: The Role of Civil Society.* Coventry: Center for the Study of Globalization and Regionalization [University of Warwick], 2003.

Rising poor and middle-income powers

"The New Titans: A Survey of the World Economy." *Economist,* September 16, 2006.

Global public opinion

Advisory Group on Public Diplomacy for the Arab and Muslim World. "Changing Minds, Winning Peace: A New Strategic Direction for U.S. Public Diplomacy in the Arab and Muslim World." Report submitted to the Committee on Appropriations, U.S. House of Representatives, October 1, 2003.

Aspen Institute. *From Values to Advocacy: Activating the Public's Support for U.S. Engagement in an Interdependent World.* Washington, DC: Aspen Institute, 2002.

Chicago Council on Foreign Relations. *Worldviews 2004: American Public Opinion and Foreign Policy.* Chicago: Chicago Council on Foreign Relations, 2004.

German Marshall Fund of the United States. "Transatlantic Trends." A Project of the German Marshall Fund of the United States and the Compagnia di San Paolo, 2002, 2003, 2004, 2005, 2006. www.transatlantictrends.org.

Global Stakeholder Panel 2020. *What NGO Leaders Want for the Year 2020: Report of the Second Survey of the Global Stakeholder Panel 2020.* Toronto, ON: 2020 Fund, 2004. www.kbs-frb.be/code/page.cfm?id_page=125&ID=437&Cnt=EN.

Norris, Pippa. "Global Governance and Cosmopolitan Citizens." In *Governance in a Globalizing World*, ed. Joseph S. Nye and John D. Donahue, 155–77. Washington, DC: Brookings Institution Press, 2000.

Telhami, Shibley. *The Stakes: America and the Middle East: The Consequences of Power and the Choice for Peace.* Boulder, CO: Westview Press, 2002.

Zogby, James J. *What Arabs Think: Values, Beliefs, and Concerns.* Utica, NY: Zogby International, 2002.

Foreign Policy Approaches

Benevolent imperialism

Fukuyama, Francis. *America at the Crossroads: Democracy, Power, and the Neo-Conservative Legacy.* New Haven: Yale University Press, 2006.

Fukuyama, Francis. "The End of History." *National Interest*, Summer 1989.

Isikoff, Michael, and David Corn. *Hubris: The Inside Story of Spin, Scandal, and the Selling of the Iraq War.* New York: Crown, 2006.

Kagan, Robert. *Of Paradise and Power: America and Europe in the New World Order.* New York: Alfred Knopf, 2003.

Odom, William E., and Robert Dujarric. *America's Inadvertent Empire.* New Haven: Yale University Press, 2004.

Ricks, Thomas E. *Fiasco: The American Adventure in Iraq.* New York: Penguin, 2006.

Woodward, Bob. *State of Denial: Bush at War, Part III.* New York: Simon & Schuster, 2006.

Nationalism

Baceyich, Andrew J. *The New American Militarism: How Americans Are Seduced by War.* New York: Oxford University Press, 2005.

"China and Japan: So Hard to Be Friends." *Economist,* March 26–April 1, 2005.

Golub, Philip S. "Dieu, la nation et l'armée, une sainte trinité." [God, Nation and Army: A Holy Trinity]. *Le Monde Diplomatique* (Paris), July 2005.

Huntington, Samuel. "The Clash of Civilizations." *Foreign Affairs* 72, no. 3 (1993): 22–49.

"In Dangerous Waters." *Economist,* October 7–13, 2006.

Lieven, Anatol. *America Right or Wrong: An Anatomy of American Nationalism.* Oxford: Oxford University Press, 2004.

Reich, Robert B. *Reason Why Liberals Will Win The Battle For America.* New York: Vintage Books, 2004.

Multilateralism

Commission on Global Governance. *Our Global Neighborhood.* Oxford: Oxford University Press, 1995.

International Commission on Intervention and State Sovereignty. *The Responsibility to Protect: The Report of the International Commission on Intervention and State Sovereignty.* Ottawa: International Development Research Center, 2001.

Kuziemko, Ilyanna, and Eric Werker. "How Much Is a Seat on the Security Council Worth? Foreign Aid and Bribery at the United Nations." *Journal of Political Economy* 114, no. 5 (October 2006): 905–30.

McGeary, Johanna. "Freedom Fighters." *Time,* March 8, 1999.

Localism

Hines, Colin. *Localization: A Global Manifesto.* London: Earthscan, 2000.

International Forum on Globalization. *Alternatives to Economic Globalization: A Better World Is Possible.* San Francisco: Berrett-Koehler, 2002.

Index